Engage Boldly. Collaborate Authentically.
Perform Relentlessly.

# THE EFFICIENT FRONTIER
# OF TEAMING

Bryan Powell & Tom Reynolds

Edited by: Kate Anslinger

# THE EFFICIENT FRONTIER OF TEAMING

## BRYAN POWELL
## TOM REYNOLDS

Edited by: Kate Anslinger

ethos
collective

Printed in the United States of America

Published by Igniting Souls
PO Box 43, Powell, OH 43065
IgnitingSouls.com

LCCN: 2025919927
Paperback ISBN: 978-1-63680-568-9
Hardcover ISBN: 978-1-63680-569-6
e-Book ISBN: 978-1-63680-570-2

Available in paperback, hardcover, e-book, and audiobook.

For Sylvia, Katin, Kylan, and Selena, and for the leaders, teams, and coaches who invited me into their real conversations. Every one of you helped shape my belief that meaningful performance always begins with how we treat one another.

—Bryan Powell

To Meghan, Josie, Ben, Mike, Pete, Mom, and Dad—the best teammates a guy like me could ask for.

—Thomas Reynolds

# TABLE OF CONTENTS

# FOREWORD

I still remember the first time I sat across from a leader who was doing everything right, and yet nothing was working.

They were smart, values-driven, and deeply committed to their people. They had invested in strategy, structure, and skill development. On paper, their team should have been thriving. But in the room, something else was present: fatigue and disconnection. There was a palpable yet quiet sense that everyone was holding back just a little of who they really were.

That moment, and thousands like it since, is why the work you are about to encounter matters so deeply to me.

At inviteCHANGE, we have spent decades listening to leaders and teams wrestle with the same essential question: *How do we perform at a high level without losing ourselves or each other in the process?* The answer has never been purely technical. It has always been human.

This book is written by leaders who understand the truth from the inside out, on the receiving end of generative coaching as team leaders and as practitioners, and who share their frontline experience with teams and their leaders around the world. An important distinction expressed in this book is that generative work does not aim to fix people or optimize them like machines. It creates the conditions where people, teams, and systems can evolve together, adaptive even in the face of great uncertainty and complexity.

## From Doing Better to Being Whole

Much of the leadership literature focuses on improvement: better communication, better accountability, better execution. These are important, but they are incomplete. They operate primarily in what we call the first two layers of the Generative Operating System™ (GOS): self-awareness and relational awareness.

Those layers ask different questions than most organizations are used to asking:

- Who am I being as I lead, beyond what am I doing?
- How do my beliefs, fears, and assumptions shape the system around me?
- What becomes possible when people feel safe enough to be real and supported enough to stretch beyond habit and preference?

This is the terrain where Generative WholenessÔ lives.

Generative WholenessÔ is not about work-life balance or self-care slogans. It is about recognizing that human beings do not check parts of themselves at the door when they enter a team or organization. Our histories, identities, emotions, and aspirations all come with us. When leaders try to manage performance without honoring that reality, they create fragmentation. When they lead with wholeness, they create energy as a compounding and positive force.

The authors of this book understand that leader and team performance are amplified by open, transparent, and modeled humanity.

## Why Teaming Is the Work of Our Time

We are living in a moment where the cost of disengagement is no longer abstract. Burnout, change fatigue, mistrust, and fragmentation are showing up everywhere, from executive teams to frontline staff. At the same time, the problems we are being asked to solve are more complex than ever.

No single leader, no matter how capable, can meet this moment alone.

That is why teaming, not just teamwork, and the intentional design of how humans collaborate, has become one of the most critical leadership capabilities of our time. And it is why this book matters.

What you will find in these pages transcends a rigid model or a set of prescriptive answers. Instead, you will encounter an invitation: to rethink how engagement and authenticity interact, how trust and accountability coexist, and how teams can move toward what the authors call an efficient frontier. That frontier has the conditions where human energy and performance reinforce each other rather than compete.

Teams are not problems to be solved; they are living systems to be cultivated. When leaders learn to notice patterns rather than assign blame, when they ask generative questions rather than impose solutions, something shifts. Conversations deepen. Ownership spreads. Performance becomes sustainable.

## Coaching as a Way of Leading

One of the things that makes me most proud as I read this work is how clearly the authors embody a coaching stance.

Generative leaders do not position themselves as the smartest person in the room. They position themselves as the stewards of the system. They listen for what is emerging, beyond what is broken. They understand that insight is co-created, not delivered.

This book reflects that posture throughout.

You will notice an absence of academic distance. Instead, there is presence. Story. Reflection. An honest reckoning with what it actually feels like to lead and belong to a team in today's world. That tone is not accidental. It is the result of deep personal work, the essential human development that begins with self-awareness and extends outward into relational and systemic impact.

That is the essence of generative leader coaching: helping leaders become, behave, and bring more of themselves while expanding their capacity to hold complexity, difference, and tension without collapsing into control.

## Engagement and Authenticity: Not a Tradeoff

One of the most persistent myths in organizational life is that leaders must choose between caring about people and driving results. This is a false choice. This is also a costly choice.

What this book makes clear is that engagement without authenticity becomes compliance, and authenticity without engagement becomes drift. Sustainable performance lives in the integration.

This mirrors what we see again and again in generative team coaching. Teams that learn to speak the truth faster, to name what is uncomfortable, and to stay connected while holding high standards do not become softer. They become stronger, more resilient, and adaptive. Ultimately, these are teams that will exercise essential creativity to be future-fit.

The efficient frontier described in this book reveals the value for leaders to pause before pushing harder, in favor of aligning energy so productive effort occurs and is no longer wasted on managing fear, politics, or unspoken tension.

## A Word to the Reader

If you are looking for a quick fix or a plug-and-play solution, this book may challenge you. It asks more of you than technique. It asks for presence, curiosity, and courage.

If you are ready to lead in a way that is both deeply human and rigorously effective, you are in the right place.

As someone who has had the privilege of walking alongside their development as generative practitioners, I can say with confidence that the insights in these pages are not theoretical. They are lived, tested, and refined in real teams with real stakes.

This work reflects the heart of the inviteCHANGE mission: to help leaders and organizations thrive by engaging the whole human system. It honors the truth that transformation does not begin with strategy. The essential evolution organizations seek begins with awareness that fully notices all that is occurring and how the system influences those choices. And from awareness, everything else becomes possible.

I am grateful you are here. I am grateful for the courage it takes to do this kind of work. And I am hopeful, deeply hopeful, that the ideas in this book will help you and your teams move closer to wholeness, connection, and performance that truly matters.

—Janet M. Harvey,
CEO & Founder inviteCHANGE

# INTRODUCTION

# The One Challenge Every Team Faces

There is no shortage of books on leadership or team development. In boardrooms, startups, and nonprofits alike, leaders are bombarded with frameworks, philosophies, and silver-bullet strategies that promise to unlock team performance. Yet the reality is sobering: most teams remain inconsistent, underdeveloped, and mired in a persistent gap between potential and performance.

In our decades of coaching and leading teams across industries, my co-author, Tom, and I kept noticing a common pattern. Teams weren't failing for lack of intelligence, talent, or intent. They were failing because they didn't know how to balance two foundational forces: **authenticity** and **engagement**. That balance, we came to believe, is the beating heart of effective teaming. And it's the focus of this book.

## The Core Problem: How to Reach the Efficient Frontier of Teaming

The central question we explore in this book is: *How can leaders move their teams toward optimal performance by intentionally balancing authenticity and engagement?*

That question led us to develop a new model, which we call **The Efficient Frontier of Teaming**. Inspired by the investment theory of the same name, our model visualizes the relationship between two vital team dynamics: the degree of authentic connection among team members (trust, psychological safety, belonging) and the level of accountability they uphold (standards, ownership, results).

Many teams over-index on one and neglect the other. Teams that emphasize only accountability can become rigid, transactional, and fear-driven. Teams that lean too heavily into authenticity risk becoming permissive, conflict-avoidant, or emotionally fragile. The most effective teams find the curve on the efficient frontier where both qualities are maximized in balance. This book is about helping leaders locate that curve and **lead their teams there**.

## Why It Matters Now

The modern workplace is under strain. Hybrid work has a fragmented connection. Burnout has chipped away at motivation. Teams are more diverse, dispersed, and digitally mediated than ever before. Under these conditions, the old models of command-and-control leadership or top-down culture change simply don't work. What teams need isn't more structure or slogans. They need leaders who understand how to guide them **through the discomfort of growth** toward sustainable, high-performance collaboration.

That growth isn't linear. It involves trust building, honest feedback, realignment, and new forms of ownership. It's not about perfection but **progress toward maturity**. Our model embraces that messiness and offers leaders a concrete path forward.

## What This Book Offers

*The Efficient Frontier of Teaming* is not a theoretical treatise. It's a practical roadmap for leaders, coaches, and practitioners who want to build stronger, more adaptive teams. Every chapter is built around:

- **Real coaching conversations** drawn from our work with teams across sectors
- **Practical tools and diagnostics** for measuring where a team is and what it needs next
- **Self-assessments and team exercises** to promote reflection and action
- **Original visual models** to frame key ideas in ways leaders can share and scale
- **Research-backed insights** that ground the book in real data

From our model of team maturity (Dependent, Collaborative, Aligned, Empowered) to our Bullseye Method for team goal setting to frameworks like the Coaching Culture Continuum, every chapter builds toward the same goal: helping your team get on and stay on the efficient frontier.

## How the Book Is Structured

The book begins with a diagnosis: what dysfunctional teams look like, how they form, and why well-intended leaders often fail to shift them. From there, we explore the spectrum of team development, providing language and examples for the stages teams progress through.

Chapters then dive into the necessary ingredients for optimal performance in teams:

- Psychological safety and trust
- Shared purpose and values
- Feedback and coaching
- Clear roles and interdependencies
- Measurable goals and learning loops

Along the way, we show what these ideas look like in real-world settings, from financial advisory firms to nonprofit boards to startup teams in crisis. In the later chapters, we explore implementation strategies: how to build a team contract, embed coaching habits into everyday meetings, use KPIs effectively without crushing morale, and keep evolving when the finish line keeps moving.

## Why This Isn't Just Another Leadership Book

This book doesn't promise one-size-fits-all answers. It offers something more powerful: **a new mental model for leading teams in complexity**. It helps leaders become coaches. It gives structure to the soft stuff and depth to the hard stuff. It invites readers to think like system builders and culture shapers, not just task managers or inspiration machines.

We didn't write this book because we thought the world needed more content on teaming. We wrote it because the world needs better **practice**. Better conversations. Better clarity. Better habits. And above all, better leaders who know that performance without connection is unsustainable—and that connection without performance is insufficient.

*The Efficient Frontier of Teaming* is our contribution to that work. It's the book we wish we had twenty years ago. And it's the book we believe will help you and your team find that next edge of possibility.

Let's begin.

# CHAPTER 1

# The Limits of Legacy Leadership

*There is beauty in what is broken.*
—K.K. Hendin

There is a trap in team leadership that many capable leaders fall into, and it's not for lack of intelligence, vision, or effort, but because of something more subtle lying beneath the surface. Teams today tend to rely on inherited models of teamwork that no longer reflect how real teams operate. I fell into that trap early in my leadership career, and it wasn't until I was forced to confront a failing team dynamic that I realized how outdated my view of team performance had become.

It was 2015. I had just stepped into a new leadership role overseeing a cross-functional wealth advisory team. We were strong on paper with individuals who were experienced, credentialed, and driven. But under the surface, something was off. We weren't aligned. Conversations in meetings felt transactional. People were courteous but rarely challenged one another's thinking. Innovation was flat. At the time, I assumed we just needed more clarity on our overall goals, defined roles, and better delegation. I doubled down on structure, efficiency, and performance reviews. The harder I pushed for execution, the more disengaged the team became.

In those days, I leaned heavily on frameworks I'd seen succeed in other corporate settings—drawn from my upbringing and my work with professional leaders—a blend of hierarchical decision-making, formal communication, and individual accountability. These models had their merits, but something critical was missing, and it was something I wouldn't fully grasp until much later: the relationship between team engagement, psychological authenticity, and sustainable performance.

That was the first time I truly began to question whether our definition of a high-performing team was too narrow, too outdated, and too disconnected from the human systems at the core of modern work. This question would eventually become the foundation for this book and the Efficient Frontier of Teaming model.

## A Personal Note on the Climb

Tom and I didn't arrive at this model from a classroom. We built it from the inside out, through years of running teams, learning from failures, and watching what happens when good people struggle in bad systems. I've seen what happens when a team gets the right nudge and starts to collaborate. We have been honored through thousands of coaching and consulting sessions to witness what can happen when a team unlocks their voice and becomes empowered. Unfortunately, we have also seen the effect and cost of teams not evolving: burnout, turnover, and mediocrity.

In one pivotal moment with my own team, we hit a wall. Deadlines were missed. Trust was eroding. Instead of pointing fingers, we paused and re-evaluated. We realigned our purpose, clarified roles, and committed to a new cadence of feedback and accountability. It was messy—but it worked. That turning point changed how I think about teaming. What you will find in this book is our attempt to chart a different path. One that is honest about the work, clear about the tools, and hopeful about what's possible when teams are built with intention. One that fits today's workplace, which has evolved to the point where face-to-face office meetings are the exception. We need new ways of thinking and behaviors that fit today's environmental challenges, especially as hybrid and remote work become more of the norm now and into the future.

Over a decade ago, I was called into my manager's office.

At the time, I had been working as a regional manager at the corporate headquarters. I had been with the company for about fourteen years, and my resume included the opening of several successful offices in the Southern California area. After much deliberation with my family, we moved to St. Louis so I could have a greater impact on the organization's leaders. At the time, the company was growing rapidly, and there was little leadership training offered at both the corporate level and the branches nationwide. I was responsible for the employees at 60 offices, guiding their performance, development, and annual reviews, while monitoring their sales productivity.

When my executive leader called me into her office, I expected to walk into a normal weekly meeting where we would rehash my staff's wins and chat about any company updates I needed to be privy to. Like most of Corporate America, this information was doled out on a need-to-know basis, dictated by the higher-ups who worked directly with the CEO.

As I sat down in the chair opposite my leader, I crossed my ankle over my knee and propped my notebook on my lap. I was ready to take notes. And she was ready for me to nod my head and go along with everything she spilled, or so I thought. But, in what I still view as a shocking turn of events, she hit me with an unexpected punch in the gut. "Bryan, we are going to hire a coach for you . . . to help you work on your leadership and communication skills," she said, matter-of-factly.

She kicked me when I was down and added, "We thought you were going to be more like other leaders on the team." Their way of doing things didn't fit my style and personality, to say the least. Instead of being focused on driving results, coaching the branch managers to perform at a higher level, and being objective in annual reviews so that leaders could improve, the other regionals were focused on where we would be going to dinner, what wine would be ordered, and cheerleading each other in how successful the team had been.

I wasn't like the other regional managers; our personalities were very different. Instead of being a positive in rounding out the team's skills, it became an obstacle that instilled the mentality that my differences were a problem. I ran with that mantra, furthering the divide.

When I look back on this experience, a couple of things resonate to this day. First, I did not feel like I had permission to be my authentic self. I was asked to show up like someone else, and the resulting unnatural feeling led me to distance myself from most of the other team members.

Secondly, my energy was drained by trying to navigate the office politics that seemed stacked against me, as sucking up was a skill some had perfected to achieve success. I want to make it clear that I didn't understand how to act in an environment where I didn't feel supported, so there were times when I openly went against the grain, adopting a sort of punk rock approach that rioted against management. Looking back, I realize this was not the right way to go.

It was after these mistakes that I began to wonder how I could have shown up differently, rather than playing the part of the outcast I felt was being thrust upon me. Ask yourself: Have I ever felt unable to show up as my authentic self? Were there times when I felt disengaged or isolated? What would have given me permission to speak up or feel that my voice would be heard? It is drawn from personal failures, missteps, and times of enlightenment that we share this framework to guide your team to reach its full potential together.

## What Legacy Models Miss

If you've ever stood atop a mountain, you know the view is only part of the story. The climb, the grinding ascent, the missteps, the recalculations, and the moments when turning back seemed easier are where the real transformation happens. Teams are much the same. We often admire peak performance from afar, marveling at the synergy and results. But what's often unseen is the path that led there: the deliberate decisions, the messy misalignments, the breakthroughs, and the quiet moments of trust forged in adversity.

This book is about that journey. It's about how teams move from being dependent on a single leader to becoming empowered, interdependent organisms capable of remarkable, sustainable performance. It's about what separates teams that simply function from those that flourish—and how leaders can architect that transition.

We live in an era where collaboration is no longer optional. In today's complex and fast-changing environment, high-functioning teams are not just a strategic advantage; they are a survival necessity. Yet many teams stall somewhere along the way. They begin with promise but get mired in confusion, siloed behaviors, or outdated leadership patterns. What they need is not just motivation, but a model for maturity.

I began reading everything I could about team dynamics.

Patrick Lencioni's *The Five Dysfunctions of a Team* offered a compelling hierarchy of challenges, focusing on qualitative attributes such as the absence of trust, fear of conflict, lack of commitment, avoidance of accountability, and inattention to results.

Simon Sinek's *Leaders Eat Last* highlighted the value of psychological safety and servant leadership.

General Stanley McChrystal's *Team of Teams* emphasized adaptability and decentralized decision-making in high-complexity environments.[1]

What resonated with me personally is that these books were smart, well-written, and often inspiring, but they didn't quite address the problem I was seeing.

They described one of two models:

1.  Fixing broken teams
2.  Thriving under very specific leadership conditions, such as in a military command, tight-knit executive units, or startup environments with shared mission statements and clarity on what they wanted to achieve in terms of delivering impact and value to the community they wanted to affect.

My challenge was more nuanced. I wasn't working with a dysfunctional or undisciplined team. I was working with good people who were operating far below their potential—not because they lacked capability, but because they weren't showing up fully.

They weren't disengaged in the typical sense. In fact, they were showing up to meetings, completing deliverables, and meeting client expectations. But there was a kind of emotional withholding I couldn't ignore. Ideas were left unsaid. Tensions went unspoken. Collaboration felt more like negotiation than co-creation. Although people were performing, individuals and team members were not growing because the environment became repetitive, focused solely on completing daily tasks and moving on to the next thing.

Think about it: Have you ever felt so engaged in your role at work that you sought out feedback, brainstormed ways to improve, or relied on each other to challenge the status quo and reach higher towards your full potential? I didn't in this situation because our results were adequate, but nothing felt truly alive or like I was inspiring positive change within the organization.

I started noticing this pattern not just in my team but across other teams I consulted with. In some cases, these teams were made up of the most talented individuals in the organization. But performance wasn't breaking through. Frustration simmered just beneath the surface. Everyone was doing their jobs, but no one was bringing their full voice. What looked like success from the outside often felt hollow within.

What I eventually came to see is that many teams operate within a narrow band of capability—not because of bad leadership or weak members, but because of what I now call **teaming inefficiency**: the gap between what a team is capable of and what it consistently delivers. And this gap isn't just about execution; it's about the conditions required for people to bring their whole selves to the work.

Creating cultures and environments where individuals are excited to participate, bring their unique strengths and skills to the team, and are not afraid to be their true selves, which, if not discussed, can lead to frustration, burnout, anxiety, and all sorts of other negative emotions. This is why I believe we are seeing some of the lowest engagement scores in over a decade, according to Gallup's annual research.

It is disappointing that we are leaving so much potential on the table. This realization that things can be done differently became the seed that led Tom and me to design the model at the foundation of this book.

## Optimal Performance vs. High Performance: Redefining What It Means to Excel as a Team

Throughout the business world, the term "high-performing team" is often used as a badge of honor. It's a label that leaders aspire to earn for their teams, consultants frequently promise to help achieve, and organizations plaster across their internal dashboards. Yet despite its popularity, the definition of high performance remains elusive, overly idealized, and often disconnected from the daily realities of modern teamwork. The term tends to conjure visions of perfect alignment, consistent top-tier results, and relentless forward momentum. But here's the truth: High performance, as it's commonly understood, often feels like an unrealistic finish line, one that few teams reach and fewer still can sustain.

In contrast, the concept of **optimal performance**, as Tom and I define it in *The Efficient Frontier of Teaming*, presents a more grounded, human-centered, and sustainable way to understand what excellence looks like in a team. Optimal performance is not about achieving perfection or reaching some static pinnacle of productivity. It's about showing up with what your team has on any given day, including its energy, cohesion, communication, trust, and capacity, and using that to its fullest potential. It's a mindset, a system, and a way of operating that prioritizes adaptability, consistency, and intentionality over unattainable ideals.

### The Problem with "High Performance" as a Goal

High-performing teams are often framed as the gold standard in business literature. Books like *The Five Dysfunctions of a Team* or *Team of Teams* highlight characteristics like deep trust, laser focus, clear accountability, and resilience under pressure. These traits are unquestionably valuable. But when "high performance" becomes a vague aspiration without definition or context, it can create more harm than good.

**It sets unrealistic expectations.** Teams may feel they are failing if they cannot sustain peak performance every day, even under changing conditions, burnout, or organizational constraints.

**It lacks adaptability.** High performance is often portrayed as a fixed destination rather than a dynamic journey. It doesn't reflect how performance must shift in response to energy, external pressures, or internal challenges.

**It ignores the human element.** Emphasizing only results can overlook the psychological, emotional, and interpersonal realities that shape performance in areas such as trust, safety, belonging, and meaning.

In many ways, high performance is like chasing the horizon. It's inspirational, but it rarely accounts for where your feet are planted today or what terrain you're walking through.

## What Is Optimal Performance?

Optimal performance, by contrast, is not about being perfect; it's about being present and intentional. It's understanding that no team brings the same resources to the table every day and that greatness lies in how you harness what you *do* have.

We define optimal performance as a team's ability to consistently operate at its full potential with the resources (such as energy, trust, communication, clarity, accountability, and engagement) available to it in the present moment.

This definition recognizes:

- **Variability:** Teams have good days and hard days. Optimal performance adapts to both.
- **Contextual intelligence:** Performance is shaped by more than just Key Performance Indicators (KPIs); it is embedded in relationships, well-being, leadership, and clarity.
- **Sustainability:** Optimal performance focuses on building a repeatable system that teams can return to and improve upon, and not just moments of brilliance.

## Table 1.1: Key Differences Between Optimal and High Performance

|  | High Performance | Optimal Performance |
|---|---|---|
| **Goal Orientation** | Outcome-driven, focused on peak results | Process- and system-driven, focused on consistency |
| **Measurement** | Based on external results (revenue, output) | Based on internal alignment and capacity utilization |
| **Sustainability** | Often unsustainable over long periods | Designed for long-term adaptability and resilience |
| **Team Experience** | Pressure to perform, often perfectionism | Empowerment to do the best with what's available |
| **Human Factors** | Often secondary or overlooked | Central to performance (trust, engagement, clarity) |

By shifting from high performance to optimal performance, we create space for teams to breathe—to adapt to their realities, to operate intentionally, and to iterate with purpose.

## Optimal Performance and the Efficient Frontier

The idea of optimal performance is at the heart of *The Efficient Frontier of Teaming*. In finance, the efficient frontier is the curve that shows the highest return you can achieve for a given level of risk. In teams, we've reimagined this as the highest level of output or effectiveness a team can achieve, given its current levels of trust, authenticity, and engagement.

Rather than pushing teams to extremes, our framework encourages teams to find their *current* efficient frontier to ask, "How can we work most effectively with what we have today?" This approach honors both the messiness and brilliance of being human at work.

The book is filled with practical ways to assess, develop, and optimize the variables that matter most: clarity of roles, strength of relationships, alignment of purpose, team communication, coaching culture, and decision-making protocols. All of these flow back to the central premise: when you design for *optimal performance*, you create the conditions for *sustained excellence*.

## A System, Not a Sprint

Too often, teams chase high performance as if it's a one-time event, such as launching a project, completing the mission, or hitting the numbers. However, truly effective teams aren't built on sprinting from win to win. They're built on a system that allows them to recover, reflect, recalibrate, and reengage.

Optimal performance is that system.

It doesn't demand that you be the best *every* day; it invites you to be your best *today*. And when your team does that over time, high performance becomes not an aspiration, but a natural outcome.

As you continue through the book, you'll notice that everything we share, whether it's the Bullseye Method, the team contract, or the teams defined in the Efficient Frontier of Teaming Trust/Accountability matrix, is designed to help teams return to their optimal performance frontier. Not once, but repeatedly.

That's the essence of our message: There is no finish line. But there is always the next best step forward, and if a team can learn to take that step together with intentionality and clarity, then optimal performance is not just possible; it's repeatable.

## The Missed Variable: Engagement × Authenticity

Most organizations evaluate team performance through result-oriented KPIs, such as output, productivity, client retention, and profitability. However, those metrics often reflect outcomes rather than the deeper mechanisms that produce them. In high-functioning teams, optimal performance isn't just the result of alignment or accountability. It's the byproduct of something deeper: sustained engagement and interpersonal authenticity.

These two dimensions—**engagement** and **authenticity**—form the axis of what we now call the *Efficient Frontier of Teaming*. Borrowing a concept from Harry Markowitz's efficient frontier in portfolio theory, which describes the optimal balance between risk and return, Tom and I apply the same logic to teams: the most effective teams operate at the frontier where performance is maximized for the level of human investment made. Anything less is wasted potential.

We often treat engagement and authenticity as cultural bonuses or "nice to have" that we can add after the work gets done. The truth is, they are the key to the team's success, and cultivating them takes time, effort, and focus. Consider the research. Google's Project Aristotle studied over 180 teams and found that the most important predictor of effectiveness wasn't seniority, intelligence, or technical skill; as it turns out, it was psychological safety.[2] This is a term that seemingly gets thrown around during HR meetings, leadership conferences, and even performance reviews with little definition or measurement of its presence in the organization's culture!

Stop and think about your personal experiences in this area. When did you feel you had permission to speak up? When did you feel that team members welcomed your thoughts, ideas, and comments?

It's inspiring to be a part of a team where this happens; however, after coaching thousands of teams, Tom and I have found that this is not the norm. Most times, in fact, it is taken for granted, or team members feel they are not empowered to contribute, which starts at the top of the organization. When asked to define what it means to be empowered by their organization, we usually see individuals look at each other, shrug, or resort to the old "looking at their phone" trick. Ha, I love that one, especially when I am presenting on stage; this trick seems older than time.

When team members felt safe to speak openly, admit mistakes, and express vulnerability, performance consistently improved. Amy Edmondson's foundational work confirmed this, defining psychological safety as "a shared belief held by members of a team that the team is safe for interpersonal risk-taking."[3] These findings resonate deeply with what I've observed in practice.

When people are engaged but inauthentic, teams become efficient but lack depth in their execution without evolution. When they are authentic but disengaged, teams become empathic but slow to trust without traction. But when both are high, performance becomes exponential. Teams generate energy, not just output.

## What the Models Don't Address

Let me be clear: Models like those in *The Five Dysfunctions* and *Team of Teams* have their place. But their strength is also their limitation. They often focus on dysfunction as the point of entry or assume that structure and alignment are sufficient to unlock higher performance. The Efficient Frontier model starts from a different premise. It assumes the team is already technically competent—but that **emotional underperformance** is the real drag on outcomes.

Whereas *The Five Dysfunctions* method treats trust as the foundation of teamwork, the Efficient Frontier framework treats **authenticity as a fuel,** which is something that expands over time and accelerates performance when engagement systems are in place. It's not enough to eliminate dysfunction; we must create the conditions for **co-elevation,** a term I borrow from Keith Ferrazzi, who describes it as the act of lifting each other while driving toward shared goals.

This framework is built on four levels of team maturity: Dependent, Collaborative, Aligned, and Empowered. Each stage represents a different relationship with engagement and authenticity. Unlike static models that apply the same tactics across all teams, this progression enables dynamic team development tailored to context, culture, and capacity.

This will be the foundation of the teaming model that Tom and I have developed through our coaching and consulting engagements with Fortune 500 organizations and smaller teams. It is a concept to understand that everyone you bring onto your team is creative, capable, and resourceful. These words were given to me by a great coaching mentor, Janet Harvey, who helped me see differently as I transitioned from being a leader to an effective coach.

In short, it is not a formula. It's a strategic path for your team to show up as their true selves and unlock the collective team's full potential.

## Why This Model Matters Now

In today's world, technical skills and strategy will only take you so far. The differentiator in complex environments is how quickly a team can learn, adapt, and mobilize. That doesn't happen by accident.

Consider the case of two project teams facing the same external crisis. One scrambles in silence, waiting for direction. The other meets quickly, revisits priorities, and reallocates work without managerial oversight.

The difference? The latter team had built psychological safety before the crisis hit. In teaming, the same principle applies: the highest-performing teams achieve extraordinary outcomes, not by avoiding all risk, but by aligning purpose, process, and people to operate near their optimal point. This frontier is not fixed; it evolves as the team grows in capability and cohesion. Getting there requires a different kind of leadership. Not command-and-control, but context-and-calibration.

In traditional models, the leader is the bottleneck or the engine. Either way, the team's performance is, in most cases, tied to the leader's presence. But in mature teams, leadership becomes a distributed asset. The leader becomes a gardener more than a general, designing the environment, nurturing growth, and clearing obstacles so others can thrive. To reach that point, however, leaders must learn to adjust. A directive style may be appropriate in early stages but becomes a hindrance if not relinquished. Similarly, too much autonomy too soon can create chaos. Effective leaders know how to diagnose the team's current level and flex accordingly.

## Curious Questions for Assessing Team Stage

- Who holds decision-making power today?
- How often do team members hold each other account-able versus relying on the leader?
- Do people speak up in meetings without fear of reprisal?
- Are leadership behaviors distributed or concentrated?
- What happens when conflict arises—avoidance, esca-lation, or resolution?

Personally, I once observed a leader who was beloved for his expertise but resisted empowering others. He felt responsible for every decision. When he finally allowed team leads to run client meetings independently with the right support structure in place, he surprisingly uncovered that it didn't cause him to lose control. He gained time, trust, and surprising momentum. It changed his role and the team's identity.

This is not just about style, it's about strategy. Your abil-ity to scale as a leader is directly tied to your ability to scale the team's capacity to lead. Focusing on increasing each team member's engagement and authenticity will fuel the organiza-tion's results, as each can bring additional energy, curiosity to help others, and ideas others might not have considered.

Stop making leadership about one individual. In the Efficient Frontier of Teaming, leadership is a collective trait we will discuss in further detail. It is time to shift the mindset so that everyone feels empowered to take ownership and hold each other accountable in a positive way.

## Teams Are Not Machines

There's a dangerous myth in many organizations that high per-formance is about eliminating friction. In this mindset, effi-ciency is king, and emotion is seen as waste. What Tom and I have witnessed with curiosity is that great teams are not lean machines going through day-to-day tasks; they are living systems. And like any living system, they require energy, feedback, rest, and connection.

Teams that perform at the efficient frontier are not conflict-free; in fact, it's quite the opposite, as they're **conflict-capable,** or what we refer to as having the energy and ability to engage in healthy debate as a unified team. Instead of avoiding hard conversations, they have found a way to metabolize them. They don't suppress differences; they recognize and appreciate them, so they channel them. They don't just "run meetings" that are seemingly unproductive; they cultivate spaces where truth can be spoken and listened to, which takes time and, more importantly, design.

As Gallup's research shows, engaged employees deliver 23 percent higher profitability and 18 percent higher productivity.[4] But engagement alone is not enough. When people are engaged but inauthentic, showing up without psychological presence, their contributions are diluted, and they shy away from sharing thoughts that could enhance innovation in an idea or process. Conversely, authenticity without engagement produces high empathy but low execution. The Efficient Frontier of Teaming occurs where both conditions are high—when people are fully present, deeply engaged, and collectively accountable.

## This Book Is Your Map

The chapters ahead will introduce a clear structure for applying this model in your team or organization. You'll find diagnostic tools, coaching strategies, and culture-building exercises. But more importantly, you'll find a mindset shift.

The truth is, most teams are not failing because they lack talent or strategy. They are underperforming because they lack the systems—and the courage—to unlock what's already present. Let's change that. Tom and I feel it's time to raise the standard of what it means to be part of a team where everyone's voice is appreciated, heard, and respected. It is time to build teams that don't just perform daily tasks but consistently innovate, collaborate, and transform the way each team member expresses their unique thoughts and ideas.

Let's raise the standard.
Let's lead differently.
Let's build teams that don't just perform but transform.

## Taking Action

- Spend time thinking about the experiences you have had in your professional career that have helped shape your thoughts and behaviors.
- Describe an experience that you have had being part of a team, either positive or negative, that you would be willing to share with your current team in an upcoming meeting.
- List at least three ideas to enhance your ability to bring your authentic self to the team. Be specific about what you need personally and how the team members could support you.
- Identify two ideas that could raise the engagement of yourself and your team members. Share these in either one-to-one conversations or in an upcoming team meeting.

# CHAPTER 2

# The Efficient Frontier of Teaming

*The strength of the team is each individual member.*
*The strength of each member is the team.*
—Phil Jackson

When it comes to teams, most organizations focus on results such as revenue growth, client retention, and speed to market. But results are outputs. To create sustainable, replicable success, leaders must focus on what drives those outcomes: the invisible forces of trust, clarity, purpose, and structure. This chapter introduces the Efficient Frontier of Teaming model, a practical and conceptual framework that helps teams navigate the balance between autonomy and alignment, performance and well-being, and structure and adaptability.

Borrowed from modern portfolio theory, the "efficient frontier" describes the optimal point at which an investor achieves the highest possible return for a given level of risk.[5] In the context of teams, this metaphor offers powerful insight. The most effective teams don't eliminate risk; they manage it skillfully through shared purpose, high trust, and distributed leadership. They build infrastructure from both a relational and an operational perspective that enables high performance under pressure.

The teams that Tom and I coach have heard the phrase "this cannot be a paint-by-numbers process" when it comes to building a team that can consistently operate at optimal performance. All too often, senior leaders try to describe an almost "kumbaya" environment where everyone is supposed to just get along. Is this realistic? Am I supposed to just do a trust fall during my workday, knowing that one of my team members will just magically appear and catch me? No, and it needs to change. Teams are all different and unique in their strengths, experience, and faults, so stop treating building your team as a "check the box" exercise.

Teams that reach the highest point of this frontier do so intentionally. They don't arrive there by accident, charisma, or hope and wishing alone. And they don't stay there without discipline. What separates these teams is not raw talent or even leadership brilliance, but a repeatable approach to development grounded in trust, mutual ownership, and adaptive structure. Everyone feels they can share their thoughts without judgment.

Think about the teams you have either been on or interacted with where one person leaves the team, and hundreds of individuals show up for their going-away party because they have become emotionally connected with that individual. This is the experience that Tom and I feel everyone should have the opportunity to find: you don't necessarily need to separate your personal self from your professional self, because you feel that who you bring to work is the same person you are at home.

## How the Theory Came to Be

In the world of investing, there are so many choices and options to fit an individual's goals, where Mr. Markowitz's work laid the foundation for what is known as risk-return optimization, which is still widely used in investment management today.[6]

Now, this book is not meant to focus on modern-day investment theory; I wouldn't want to bore you with those details. The focus on the Efficient Frontier of Teaming correlates to how Tom and I approach conversations with teams and their leaders. There are so many different combinations of leader personalities, team member strengths, and focuses (or lack thereof) on measurements of success and other attributes that we will discuss throughout this book.

Both of us are self-proclaimed coaching geeks and enjoy reading about different concepts that can elevate both personal and team performance. However, one thing we have found missing is that most resources focus on theories without providing much guidance on how to apply what is learned to their teams.

We have made a considered effort to ensure this book provides stories, structure, and tools you can take back, whether you are currently leading a team or a member of a team that still has work to do to reach its full potential.

Let's review the framework together to set the foundation of the journey you are about to embark on throughout this book.

## From Functional to High-Performing

Most teams are not broken. They are not looking for someone to come in and "fix" them. They are simply underdeveloped. They hit their goals, maintain civility, and avoid major issues, although they're not learning, growing, or harnessing the full capacity of their people. They're efficient but not effective.

If I had a quarter for every time a leader or team communicated that they were "at capacity," I wouldn't need to show up to work tomorrow. When we can take an honest look, it is interesting to see the disconnect between fantasy and reality.

For example, we have both had numerous coaching conversations with senior leaders who paint a Picasso-like picture of beauty and intrigue: their team appreciates each other's company, has high trust, and enjoys every interaction together. Team members have shared that it feels more like a Stephen King novel, where they are afraid to look above their cubicle or open a shut door for fear of what might happen next.

In one such coaching engagement with a large wealth advisory organization, we identified at the beginning that processes were sound, people were capable, and results were respectable, though something was missing. Feedback was infrequent. Innovation moved at a snail's pace, and meetings were performative, with team members showing up like clockwork, except with little contribution.

How could this happen with a dozen talented professionals who understood their individual roles working side by side? Collaboration within the team was scarce, if not nonexistent, in some cases. Associates deferred to partners, partners worked in silos, and decisions bottlenecked at the top. On paper, they were succeeding. In reality, they were stuck.

What changed wasn't strategy; we've both seen teams competent at completing tasks, putting out fires, and checking off the boxes in their job descriptions. It was culture. We began by introducing open forums where, regardless of seniority, each team member could challenge assumptions, engage in healthy debate, and pitch new ideas. We mapped decision rights and clarified their purpose beyond profitability.

Slowly, the tone shifted. Within months, the team launched new services, improved client engagement, and doubled internal referrals. They didn't just work better; they worked together.

## The Teaming Inefficiency Gap

If you've ever looked at your team and thought, "We're doing fine, but we should be doing more," you've sensed what Tom and I call the **teaming inefficiency gap**. This is the space between the team's visible performance and its latent potential. It's not about burnout or disengagement. It's about underutilized insight, hidden tension, and unspoken contribution, and it's far more common than most leaders realize.

According to research by McKinsey & Company, only about 21 percent of executives report that their strategies satisfactorily meet multiple quality tests, which underscores how few leadership teams feel confident about strategy execution and delivery.[7] Yet these same teams score highly on technical competence and experience. The gap lies in *how* they work together, not *what* they know.

We often assume that if team members are aligned on goals, good execution will follow. But alignment without relational trust becomes brittle. And trust without a clear shared language becomes inconsistent. Bridging the teaming inefficiency gap requires more than off-sites or assessments. It requires a new framework for understanding team performance and not just as output, but as a **human system** of energy, trust, and commitment in motion.

In studying teams that consistently outperform their peers not just for a quarter, but year over year, Tom and I have noticed five behavioral patterns that distinguish them. These aren't tactics. They're embedded practices:

1. **They speak the truth faster.** They don't wait for a quarterly review to surface issues. There's an ongoing culture of candor.
2. **They build micro-trust daily.** Small gestures of acknowledgment, vulnerability, and follow-through are recognized as foundational and embedded in the DNA of the team.
3. **They manage tension rather than avoid it.** Conflict isn't suppressed; it's channeled into shared goals. Being able to engage in "healthy debate" is exciting, knowing

we will be able to innovate and create at the highest level.

4. **They revisit their purpose frequently.** Mission alignment isn't a one-time activity. It's a rhythm.
5. **They make space for the whole person.** Authenticity is not a liability; it's a differentiator.

These behaviors closely correlate with what Google's Project Aristotle, Amy Edmondson, and Gallup have been telling us for years: psychological safety, meaningful engagement, and identity alignment are not just culture metrics; they drive team performance. Just because they are qualitative does not mean we cannot measure them or that they do not affect the execution of the quantitative goals teams hear about daily.

## The Teaming Inefficiency Gap

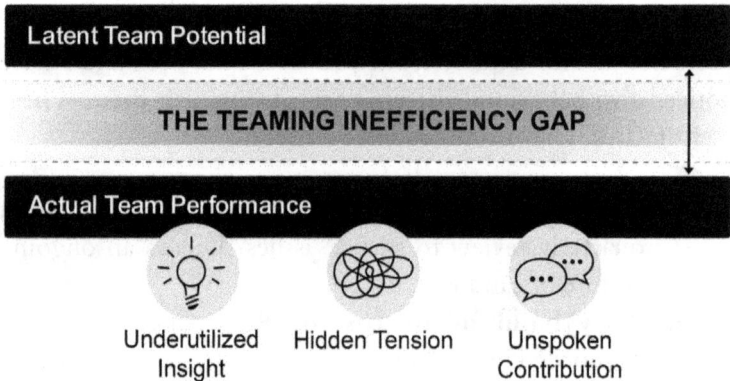

Figure 2.1: The Teaming Inefficiency Gap

## The Two Levers That Matter Most

I remember standing at the whiteboard during a leadership retreat with a team I was coaching. They were trying to redesign their client service process after months of internal confusion and misaligned communication, trying to figure it out with my assistance. Everyone agreed on the objective, but the team couldn't seem to move forward.

One of our senior team members, usually quiet and compliant, finally said, "We keep changing the workflow, but no one's saying what really needs to be said." It landed like a lightning bolt in the room. The conversation paused. People shifted in their chairs. She continued, "We've stopped being honest about what's not working. Everyone's nodding, but no one's speaking up."

That was the moment I realized process alone won't fix performance. Until people feel safe to show up authentically—and are energized enough to care deeply—the system can't improve. You can't build high-functioning teams without engaging the human levers underneath the surface.

Those two levers—**authenticity** and **engagement**— became the core of everything we began to change.

## What Are We Actually Pulling?

There are countless frameworks for managing teams, and many of them focus on surface-level behaviors: communicate more clearly, define roles, and align on goals. All valid. But the question most leaders fail to ask is: *What human conditions are necessary for these behaviors to succeed in the first place?*

What we've found, both through research and lived experience, is that most team interventions fail because they optimize systems without addressing the emotional infrastructure. People nod through team meetings, repeat company values, and even participate in off-sites while remaining emotionally checked out or psychologically guarded. That's because traditional models optimize for alignment. But performance is not just a function of alignment; it's a function of aliveness.

Teams thrive when two fundamental capacities are present and mutually reinforcing:

1. **Engagement:** the level of focused energy, effort, and emotional commitment individuals bring to the team.
2. **Authenticity:** the degree to which individuals feel safe and invited to express themselves fully, including truth-telling, risk-taking, and vulnerability.

You can have engagement without authenticity (think of fast-moving but politically cautious teams). You can also have authenticity without engagement (think of teams that connect deeply but struggle to ship). But only when both are high does a team consistently produce innovation, adaptability, and resilience.

## Engagement Without Authenticity

Let's start with a story. A high-growth fintech firm hired us to work with its strategy team. They were described as sharp, focused, and "always on." When we met them, the energy in the room was unmistakable. Laptops were open, people were multitasking even during introductions, and the velocity of conversation was high. But as we went deeper, something strange happened.

During an exercise in which we asked team members to simply define trust on the team, one team member hesitated before sharing. "It's weird," he said. "We're all dialed in, but I feel like I have to keep my guard up all the time. It's not that I don't like my teammates. I just don't know if honesty is welcome here." It was a team driven by performance but allergic to vulnerability. They were high on engagement, but low on authenticity.

This pattern isn't rare. Many elite teams, especially in high-stakes industries like finance, law, or tech, build a culture of execution but suppress emotional honesty. People learn to say what's safe. Dissent is packaged in ambiguity. Conflict is avoided or buried. Energy is high, but trust is conditional.

What results is a kind of emotional erosion. Over time, people begin to protect themselves. Burnout creeps in. Decision quality declines. The team delivers, but it costs them.

## Authenticity Without Engagement

Now flip the script. A nonprofit leadership team I coached had deep interpersonal trust. They cared for each other. Meetings began with personal check-ins. People shared openly. Vulnerability was welcomed. But when it came time to execute on strategy, they struggled. "I know I can be myself here," one director told me. "But sometimes it feels like we avoid urgency. We spend more time discussing than doing."

In this case, the team had created an emotionally support-ive environment, but lacked the focused drive to challenge one another, commit decisively, and follow through with discipline.

When teams prioritize psychological safety without rein-forcing purpose, standards, or urgency, they risk becoming insular. Conflict becomes too uncomfortable. Feedback gets softened. The mission fades into the background. Engagement is the missing ingredient that turns potential into action.

## The Efficient Frontier Zone

The best teams don't trade authenticity for engagement or vice versa. They invest in both. They live in the tension of truth and traction.

In these teams:

- People speak up *and* show up.
- Conversations are real *and* respectful.
- Performance is measured *and* meaningful.

This is the **Efficient Frontier of Teaming,** the edge where human potential meets sustained excellence. And it's not theoretical. Teams that reach this zone outperform in measurable ways.

According to Gallup, organizations with high employee engagement and high psychological safety see:

- 64 percent lower safety incidents
- 41 percent lower absenteeism
- 59 percent less turnover
- 21 percent higher profitability[8]

These aren't just culture metrics. They're business outcomes.

Amy Edmondson's foundational work showed that teams with high psychological safety not only learn faster, but they also make fewer mistakes and recover from them more effectively.[9] In environments where both engagement and authenticity are high, teams become self-correcting systems. They don't just function, they evolve.

Let's define the terms more clearly.

**Engagement** is not just motivation. It's:

- Purpose alignment (Do I care about what we're doing?)
- Cognitive presence (Am I mentally focused on the work?)

- Emotional commitment (Do I feel connected to the team?)
- Behavioral follow-through (Am I consistent and accountable?)

Engagement answers the question: *Am I here with energy and intention?*

**Authenticity** is not just "being yourself." It's:

- Psychological safety (Can I speak honestly without fear?)
- Self-expression (Do I feel seen for who I am?)
- Relational transparency (Are we telling each other the truth?)
- Value congruence (Can I act in alignment with what matters to me?)

Authenticity answers the question: *Can I show up as the real me—and will that make us better?*

Once you start looking through this lens, you begin to see teams differently. They're not mechanical units. They're human systems. And like all human systems, they carry history, emotion, memory, and identity. A mechanical team operates like a machine: Inputs → process → output. The goal is predictability. Emotions are noise. Relationships are secondary.

A human team, by contrast, is dynamic. Trust shifts. Energy fluctuates. Norms evolve. More than just efficiency, these teams require **attunement** from all of the team members. Leaders must pay attention not just to what's getting done, but also to *how people are experiencing the work.*

That's the central insight of this book: **you can't separate performance from psychology.** And when you stop trying to, better results follow.

## Introducing the Efficient Frontier of Teaming Model

The four team types, as mapped on the Efficient Frontier, are:

- **Dependent Team** – Low Engagement, Low Authenticity
- **Collaborative Team** – Low Engagement, High Authenticity
- **Aligned Team** – High Engagement, Low Authenticity
- **Empowered Team** – High Engagement, High Authenticity

Let's explore each one in depth.

## The Efficient Frontier Is a Journey, Not a Destination

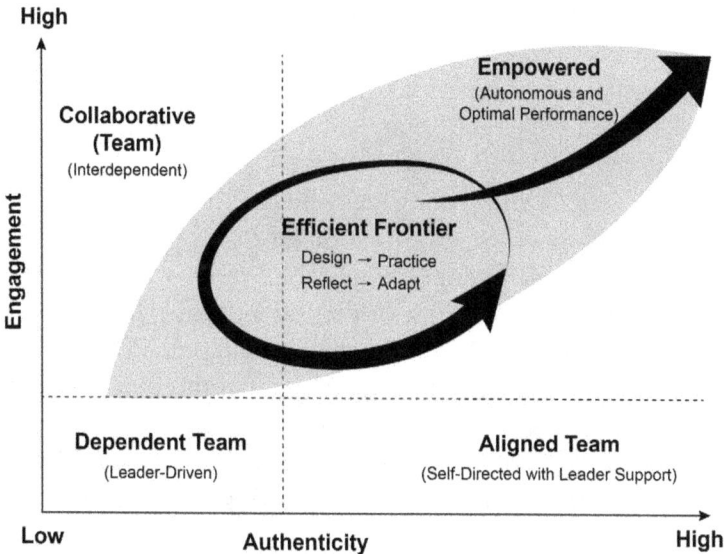

Figure 2.2: The Efficient Frontier of Teaming

## 1. The Dependent Team: Low Engagement, Low Authenticity

This team is driven primarily by **authority**, not shared owner-ship. Members rely heavily on the leader for direction, approval, and problem-solving. Meetings are passive. Risk-taking is low. Communication tends to flow top-down.

You'll often hear phrases like:

- "Just tell me what you want me to do."
- "I don't want to step on anyone's toes."
- "That's not my responsibility."

The Dependent Team is not necessarily toxic, but it is fragile. These teams are vulnerable to burnout, turnover, and inertia. When the leader is unavailable or unclear, productivity often grinds to a halt. Mistakes go unreported. Initiative is rare.

I once coached a regional office of a national firm whose team seemed polite and compliant, though disconnected from one another. When I asked how feedback was handled, one associate said, "Oh, we don't really do that here. You just learn by not getting yelled at." Engagement surveys showed low energy, but no one was speaking up.

This is the quiet danger of dependent teams: **low authenticity masks low engagement**, creating a façade of order that hides stagnation underneath. Moving out of this phase requires a deliberate investment in both **safety** and **voice**. Team members need to be invited repeatedly to share ideas, take initiative, and speak truth without penalty, knowing that everyone has each other's best interest at heart.

## 2. The Collaborative Team: High Authenticity, Low Engagement

These teams are often described as **supportive** and **close-knit**. Members trust each other, share openly, and value personal connection. But despite their strong relationships, their output is inconsistent. They hesitate to make hard decisions. Accountability is uneven.

You'll hear:

- "We get along great, but we're still behind."
- "We talked about it . . . again."
- "I didn't want to push—it felt like bad timing."

This team thrives on connection but struggles with **momentum**. Their caution stems from a desire not to damage relationships.

Sometimes they conflate care with consensus, assuming that disagreement threatens cohesion.

The Collaborative Team can be a beautiful place to work, and for some, it can be incredibly frustrating. Leaders in this phase often say, "I love this team, but I'm tired of doing all the heavy lifting."

Tom and I have seen this team type emerge frequently in nonprofit boards, community-led initiatives, and founder-led companies transitioning from startup to scale. The organization's culture is rooted in values, but those values haven't been translated into **execution rhythms or performance habits**. The work in this phase involves building clarity: clearer goals, decision rights, and follow-through systems. But it must be done **without sacrificing trust,** or the authenticity that makes the team special will collapse under structure.

## 3. The Aligned Team: Low Authenticity, High Engagement

The Aligned Team is focused, energetic, and goal-driven. These teams often achieve results. They meet deadlines. They perform under pressure. There's a shared understanding of roles and accountability.

But there's also **an edge of reservation**. People are thoughtful, although they remain cautious. Conflict is navigated, not explored. Differences are respected but not fully leveraged, and feedback is mostly one-directional, from the top down.

You'll hear:

- "We're doing well—but it doesn't always feel great."
- "I wish we had more space to challenge ideas."
- "We hit the number—but missed the meaning."

This team thrives on execution but struggles with emotional range. They value progress and focus mostly on ensuring lagging

KPIs are accomplished, but are limited by partial truths, as on this type of team, spreadsheets can direct where they prioritize their time. As long as results stay strong, these teams look successful, although when adversity hits, such as when they experience unexpected turnover, client loss, or market shifts, the cracks can appear, and they can crumble under the weight of unprocessed tension.

One wealth advisory team I worked with had strong AUM growth and glowing client reviews. But during a merger process, deep unspoken tensions surfaced. Leaders were surprised when trusted team members suddenly left. The problem wasn't performance; it was **emotional disconnection**.

The way forward here is to **expand safety without lowering standards**. Leaders must model vulnerability. Challenge must be welcomed, not avoided. Listening must be active, not performative.

## 4. The Empowered Team: High Engagement, High Authenticity

This is the Efficient Frontier in motion. The Empowered Team performs **not because they are perfect**, but because they have created conditions that support resilience, honesty, and drive. They challenge each other without diminishing each other. They act with urgency without compromising care for each other. They experiment, iterate, and learn as they go.

In these teams, you'll hear:

- "What am I missing?"
- "Can we talk about what didn't work?"
- "How can I support your growth this quarter?"

There's a balance of autonomy and alignment. People own outcomes and not just their individual tasks. They always speak up, not just when asked, because they feel their voices are welcome, as their ideas make meaningful contributions to accomplishing the team's goals. They take responsibility not just for what they do, but for **how the team feels**.

These teams are rare, but they are not mythical creatures, though you might spot a unicorn before being a part of one of these teams. They emerge when leaders commit to building both engagement and an authenticity *systemically*, not situationally.

And the result? Teams that don't just survive challenges but evolve because of them. They welcome the challenge of creating new processes together. They support each other when obstacles appear. They are there to support their team members' success, not just their own.

## Table 2.1: Dependent Teams vs. Empowered Teams

| Dimension | Functional Teams | Empowered Frontier Teams |
|---|---|---|
| Trust | Polite, guarded | Vulnerable, candid, open |
| Accountability | Leader-enforced | Peer-driven, mutual |
| Purpose | Present but passive | Active filter for decisions |
| Decision-Making | Centralized | Contextual, shared |
| Leadership | Positional | Situational and distributed |
| Feedback Culture | Formal, infrequent | Continuous, built-in |
| Innovation | Sporadic | Embedded in workflow |

## The Journey Between Them

It's easy to treat these four team types as boxes to check, although they are better understood as **waypoints** on a journey. Teams can move forward or backward due to leadership changes, cultural shifts, or major events.

For example:

- A Collaborative Team may evolve into an Empowered Team by embracing structured accountability.
- An Aligned Team may regress to Dependent after a difficult reorganization if psychological safety is eroded.
- A Dependent Team may leap forward into Collaborative through intentional trust-building and vulnerability exercises.

The goal is not perfection. It's **progress**.

One of the most important truths about this model is that team development is **not linear**. Teams don't move step by step like a staircase. Sometimes they take two steps forward and one step back. Sometimes one part of the team evolves faster than another. What matters most is that leaders recognize where their teams are and choose to lead **the team they have,** not the one they wish they had. This is where diagnostic tools, honest dialogue, and structured feedback become essential. Without a clear view of the current state, there's no path forward.

# Seeing Where You Are on the Journey

## The Efficient Frontier of Teaming Diagnostic

One of the quiet truths about teams is that most of them already know there is more possible. They feel it in productive meetings that are oddly draining. In decisions that get made yet never fully land. In results that look strong on paper, while energy quietly leaks out of the system. Teams are rarely confused about where they want to go. They want clarity. Trust. Momentum. They want to feel proud not only of what they produce, but of how they work together. What they struggle with is naming where they are right now and how much that gap matters.

When teams cannot see themselves clearly, they compensate. Leaders add structure. New processes appear. Accountability tightens. Team members work harder, stay polite, and tell themselves this is simply the cost of performance. But effort without orientation is exhausting. Over time, it erodes both results and relationships. Tom and I have sat with countless leadership teams who believed the problem was strategy, communication, or motivation. Almost without exception, when we slowed the conversation down, something deeper surfaced. The team was not broken. It was simply operating under a set of conditions that no longer matched the work's requirements. That is what it means to be between stages.

The Efficient Frontier of Teaming Diagnostic exists for this exact moment. Not to judge teams. Not to label them. But to help them pause long enough to see the pattern of how they are actually working together. Once that pattern is visible, teams can stop guessing and start making intentional choices about what to strengthen next.

## The Four Core Conditions Behind Every Team

Every team, regardless of size, industry, or performance level, is shaped by four core conditions. These conditions are always present. Teams do not earn them or graduate into them. They simply reflect the environment created by how people lead, relate, execute, and take ownership together.

**Direction and Leadership** is about clarity. It shows up in how priorities are set, how decisions are made, and how leadership is exercised across the system. Early on, leadership often needs to be more directive. As teams mature, leadership becomes more shared and situational. What matters is not the style, but whether leadership creates movement or dependence.

**Trust and Authenticity** is about psychological safety and truth-telling. It is reflected in whether people feel safe speaking honestly, admitting mistakes, and challenging one another without fear. Many teams confuse the absence of conflict with trust. In reality, silence is often a sign that people are editing themselves to stay safe.

**Alignment and Accountability** is about execution. It includes clear roles, shared expectations, and follow-through. Strong alignment creates momentum. Weak alignment creates confusion. Alignment without trust can feel rigid. Trust without alignment can feel unfocused. Teams need both.

**Ownership and Adaptability** is about initiative and learning. It reflects whether people feel responsible for the success of the whole team, not just their role. It also shows up in how quickly teams learn, adjust, and respond as conditions change. Ownership is not about working harder. It is about caring deeply enough to act.

Every team lives inside all four conditions at the same time. Teams struggle when one condition matures faster than the others. Teams thrive when they develop together.

This is why the diagnostic looks at all four simultaneously.

## How to Complete the Diagnostic

Each team member completes the diagnostic individually, responding based on lived experience rather than aspiration.

Use the following scale:

- 1 means strongly disagree
- 2 means disagree
- 3 means sometimes or inconsistent
- 4 means agree
- 5 means strongly agree

There are no right answers. The value of this diagnostic is honesty.

## The Efficient Frontier of Teaming Diagnostic

### Direction and Leadership

1. Our team has clear priorities that guide daily decisions.
2. When decisions are needed, we know who has the authority to make them.
3. Leadership expectations are clear, even when leadership shifts by situation.
4. The team continues to move forward when the formal leader is unavailable.
5. Direction is communicated clearly rather than assumed.
6. Team members understand how their work connects to the bigger picture.
7. Leadership behaviors model what is expected from the rest of the team.
8. Decisions are explained rather than simply announced.

9. The team can act without waiting for permission on everything.
10. Leadership feels enabling rather than controlling.
11. Leadership responsibility is shared when appropriate.
12. The team knows when leadership should be centralized and when it should be distributed.

## Trust and Authenticity

13. Team members feel safe speaking up even when their view differs.
14. Mistakes can be discussed without fear of blame.
15. People feel comfortable being themselves on this team.
16. Difficult topics are addressed rather than avoided.
17. Feedback is delivered with honesty and care.
18. Team members listen to understand rather than defend.
19. Disagreement does not damage relationships on the team.
20. People are open about challenges, not just successes.
21. It feels acceptable to say I do not know or I need help.
22. Trust on this team feels real rather than performative.
23. People believe candor will be met with respect.
24. Team members do not fear negative consequences for speaking honestly.

## Alignment and Accountability

25. Roles and responsibilities are clearly defined.
26. The team consistently follows through on commitments.
27. Goals are clear and revisited regularly.
28. Performance expectations are understood by everyone.
29. Accountability conversations happen when needed.
30. The team holds itself to high standards.
31. Meetings result in clear decisions and next steps.
32. Progress is measured in meaningful ways.

33. Team members hold each other accountable, not just the leader.
34. Results are talked about openly.
35. Missed commitments are addressed rather than ignored.
36. Standards are enforced consistently across the team.

## Ownership and Adaptability

37. Team members take initiative beyond their formal roles.
38. People feel ownership for the success of the whole team, not just their own work.
39. The team adapts effectively when conditions change.
40. Learning from experience is part of how the team operates.
41. Feedback is used to improve rather than defend.
42. Team members support each other's growth and development.
43. Problems are addressed proactively rather than reactively.
44. The team reflects on what is working and what is not.
45. New ideas are encouraged and explored.
46. The team learns faster today than it did six months ago.
47. Responsibility does not stop at role boundaries.
48. The team experiments and adjusts rather than clinging to old solutions.

## Scoring the Diagnostic

Each condition includes twelve questions, producing a score between **12 and 60**.

- 12–28: Fragile or inconsistent
- 29–40: Present but uneven
- 41–52: Strong but not yet embedded
- 53–60: Embedded and consistently demonstrated

What matters is not a single score, but the pattern across all four.

## Authenticity and Engagement: The Forces Behind the Frontier

Up to this point, the diagnostic has asked you to look at four conditions independently. But teams do not experience these conditions in isolation. They interact. They reinforce one another. And when you step back far enough, a clearer pattern begins to emerge.

Those four conditions organize into two deeper forces that shape how teams actually function: **authenticity** and **engagement**. Understanding this distinction is critical because most teams do not stall due to a lack of effort or capability. They stall because one of these forces has outpaced the other.

### Authenticity

*Can people show up fully, honestly, and safely?*

Authenticity answers a simple but powerful question:

Is it safe and meaningful for me to bring my real perspective, concerns, and ideas into this team?

Two of the diagnostic conditions primarily measure authenticity.

**Trust and Authenticity** reflects the emotional and psychological foundation of the team. It captures psychological safety, truth-telling, comfort with vulnerability, and the willingness to speak up. When this condition is weak, authenticity is constrained regardless of how strong the team appears in other areas.

**Ownership and Adaptability** reflects whether authenticity is being acted on rather than merely felt. Ownership shows up when people take initiative, step beyond role boundaries, learn from mistakes, and experiment without fear. In this sense, ownership is authenticity in motion. It is what happens when people feel safe enough to care and capable enough to act.

Together, Trust and Ownership form the **authenticity foundation** of the team.

### Engagement

*Are people meaningfully invested, aligned, and contributing toward shared outcomes?*

Engagement answers a different but equally important question: Do I understand the work, believe in it, and feel responsible for moving it forward?

Two of the diagnostic conditions primarily measure engagement.

**Direction and Leadership** provides the structural container for engagement. It reflects clarity of priorities, decision authority, and leadership behaviors that enable contribution. Without direction, engagement scatters. With it, effort becomes focused and purposeful.

**Alignment and Accountability** reflects whether engagement is sustained and reinforced. It shows up in follow-through, peer accountability, role clarity, and execution discipline. Engagement without accountability becomes enthusiasm without impact. Accountability converts intention into results.

Together, Direction and Alignment form the **engagement foundation** of the team.

### Seeing the Pattern

When you look at your scores through this lens, the diagnostic becomes more than a snapshot. It becomes a compass. Teams with high engagement but low authenticity often look productive while quietly becoming dependent or disengaged. Teams with high authenticity but uneven engagement often feel supportive but struggle to gain traction. Teams that perform at the highest level develop both forces together.

The Efficient Frontier of Teaming is not about choosing between authenticity and engagement. It is about recognizing that optimal performance emerges when both mature in balance.

With this lens in place, the four types of teams become easier to see and easier to understand. The scores tell a story. And that story reveals not only where your team is today, but what must develop next for the journey to continue.

## How the Scores Reveal the Four Types of Teams

### Seeing the Story Behind the Numbers

The purpose of the diagnostic is not classification. It is orientation. Your scores are not a verdict on your team. They are a snapshot of the conditions your team is currently creating together. When you read them as a pattern rather than isolated numbers, a story begins to emerge.

That story explains how your team is functioning today and, more importantly, what must shift for the team to move forward on the Efficient Frontier of Teaming.

## Dependent Team

**Strong direction, limited shared ownership**

**Typical Score Pattern**

- Direction and Leadership: 41–60
- Trust and Authenticity: 12–40
- Alignment and Accountability: 29–40
- Ownership and Adaptability: 12–40

**Example Results**

- Direction 54, Trust 31, Alignment 36, Ownership 28
- Direction 46, Trust 26, Alignment 39, Ownership 33

### What This Tells Us

In a Dependent Team, leadership is doing the heavy lifting. Direction is clear. Decisions get made. Progress happens. From the outside, the team may even appear stable or successful.

But the diagnostic reveals what is happening underneath. Lower scores in Trust and Ownership suggest that team members are relying on leadership rather than stepping forward themselves. Initiative is cautious. Candor is selective. People wait to be asked rather than offering perspective proactively. This is not a failure of leadership. It often emerges because leadership is strong and well-intentioned. The unintended consequence is that the system learns to depend.

### What This Team Must Work on Next

Movement forward does not require more direction. It requires shared ownership and psychological safety. The work here is to invite voice, encourage initiative, and normalize learning rather than perfection. Leaders must resist the urge to fill every gap and instead create space for others to step into it. The move from Dependent to Collaborative begins when trust and ownership are intentionally developed, not when leadership works harder.

## Collaborative Team

**High trust, uneven traction**

**Typical Score Pattern**

- Direction and Leadership: 29–40
- Trust and Authenticity: 41–60
- Alignment and Accountability: 12–40
- Ownership and Adaptability: 29–40

**Example Results**

- Direction 35, Trust 52, Alignment 30, Ownership 34
- Direction 31, Trust 44, Alignment 26, Ownership 39

### *What This Tells Us*

Collaborative Teams feel good to be part of. Relationships are strong. People listen. There is openness, care, and psychological safety.

The scores reveal that execution is struggling to keep pace with trust. Lower Alignment scores point to unclear roles, inconsistent follow-through, or discomfort holding peers accountable. Decisions may be inclusive but slow. Conversations may be honest but inconclusive.

## What This Team Must Work on Next

To move forward, this team must strengthen alignment and accountability without sacrificing trust.

Clarifying roles, setting explicit standards, and normalizing accountability as an act of care is the work here. Collaborative Teams move up the Efficient Frontier when they learn that accountability deepens trust rather than threatening it.

## Aligned Team

### Strong execution, limited candor

### Typical Core Pattern

- Direction and Leadership: 41–60
- Trust and Authenticity: 29–40
- Alignment and Accountability: 41–60
- Ownership and Adaptability: 29–52

### Example Results

- Direction 55, Trust 34, Alignment 53, Ownership 41
- Direction 45, Trust 29, Alignment 46, Ownership 38

## What This Tells Us

Aligned Teams deliver. Expectations are clear. Standards are high. Results are consistent.

What lags is authenticity. Feedback is filtered. Tension is managed quietly. Over time, performance remains strong while engagement quietly erodes.

## *What This Team Must Work on Next*

The work is not more structured. It is deeper psychological safety and truth-telling. Aligned Teams become Empowered Teams when candor becomes as strong as execution.

## Empowered Team

### Balanced strength across all four conditions

### Typical Score Pattern

- Direction and Leadership: 41–60
- Trust and Authenticity: 41–60
- Alignment and Accountability: 41–60
- Ownership and Adaptability: 41–60

### Example Results

- Direction 52, Trust 49, Alignment 54, Ownership 46
- Direction 57, Trust 53, Alignment 48, Ownership 51

## *What This Tells Us*

Empowered Teams are not perfect. They are balanced.

Leadership is clear but shared. Trust is resilient. Accountability is peer-driven. Ownership extends beyond roles.

## *What This Team Must Work on Next*

The work is maintenance and renewal. Context always changes. Balance must be actively sustained.

## The Coaching Insight That Changes Everything

This is the moment to slow down and take in what you are seeing.

Teams do not stall because they lack talent, intelligence, or commitment. Most teams are filled with capable people who care deeply about the work and about one another. What causes teams to stall is not effort. It is imbalance.

One condition matures faster than the others.
Strong leadership without shared ownership creates dependence.
High trust without accountability creates drift.
Strong execution without authenticity creates quiet disengagement.
High ownership without clarity creates chaos.

None of these patterns means a team is failing. They mean a team has grown unevenly.

That distinction matters because it changes how leaders respond. When teams feel stuck, the instinct is to apply pressure everywhere. Add structure. Push harder. Move faster. The diagnostic invites a different response. It shows you where the system is compensating and where it is constrained.

The numbers are not the point. The pattern is.

This assessment does not tell you what to fix in general. It tells you where to focus first. Growth does not come from pressure. It comes from precision.

Before you move forward, pause.

Complete the diagnostic honestly. Write down your four scores. Place them into the scoring matrix and sit with what you see. Notice which condition is carrying the team and which one is quietly limiting it.

If you are doing this work as a team, complete the diagnostic independently first. Do not rush to agreement. Differences are not noise. They are signals. They reveal how the team is experienced, not how it hopes to be experienced.

## Final Thoughts: Building the Conditions

The Efficient Frontier of Teaming is not a fixed point. As your team grows in capacity and cohesion, the frontier expands. But reaching it requires more than talent; it requires intention. Structure must support trust. Accountability must be mutual. Leadership must evolve from control to cultivation. The teams that thrive aren't simply executing well, as that has become table stakes. They are thinking systemically, leading adaptively, and collaborating with honesty, vulnerability, and courage because they are designed for performance and resilience.

Consider these questions to assess your current team state.

1. Do team members regularly give and receive honest feedback?
2. Are decisions made collaboratively or funneled through one person?
3. Is psychological safety visible, and do people challenge and contribute freely?
4. Are mistakes treated as learning opportunities or liabilities?
5. Is leadership distributed or concentrated?
6. Is your stated purpose actively used to guide choices?

Scoring consistently on the frontier side indicates maturity and readiness. Low or mixed scores point to transitional work that the team may need to discuss.

## Taking Action

- Review the four different types of teams identified along The Efficient Frontier of Teaming. Where would you currently plot your team and why?
- Discuss with your team what authenticity means to you and where your ideas would allow you to bring more of your unique self to your role.
- Hold a meeting together as a team to identify at least two to three areas that you believe would enhance the overall engagement of the team.
- Review the results of the team diagnostic tool and game plan as a team on which drivers of performance would give the team the biggest lift between authenticity and engagement.

# CHAPTER 3

## One Team, Many Thoughts: Celebrating the Differences of Thought and Experience

*Strength lies in differences, not in similarities.*
—Stephen Covey

### Introduction: Appreciating the Strengths of Individuals

When leaders describe the teams that they want to build in the future, the words are often the same: high-performing, collaborative, and agile. The vision sounds compelling, inspiring, and almost universal. However, when you ask them to define how they'll achieve this, the conversation often drifts into vague aspirations about culture and mindset. Rarely does anyone admit the truth: they prefer to work with people who think, act, and communicate exactly as they do.

That's the hidden tension of teamwork. We say we value diverse thought, but we're wired to seek familiarity. The psychological pull of the similarity effect shows that we tend to gravitate toward those who resemble us, which can be powerful, as it provides insight into how some teams are created, even unintentionally, to look the same. It feels easier to build trust with people who validate our ideas. But the cost of surrounding ourselves with sameness is steep: complacency, blind spots, and missed opportunities.

When Tom and I reflect on the hundreds of leadership teams we've supported, we've noticed a pattern: many teams never tap into their full potential because they fail to appreciate, understand, and integrate their differences. This chapter is an invitation to break that cycle.

## The Hidden Bias of Sameness

In one coaching engagement, I was asked to come in and conduct an off-site for a team, which Tom and I both do quite often. We can use different assessment tools to identify team members' personalities and map their strengths. This fantastic team is a trust company that provides value and impact to its clients. When I revealed the results of mapping the team's strengths, Michelle, the team's leader, could now see that the organization was hiring team members who were so similar to each other.

You see, nearly every team member shared a similar profile: collaborative, relational, and harmony-seeking. They excelled at creating a supportive environment but struggled to make hard decisions or challenge assumptions.

As Michelle studied the map, she laughed uncomfortably. "I've basically hired a team of people who work exactly like me," she said. You can see her team's map below, created after everyone on the team completed a DISC assessment.

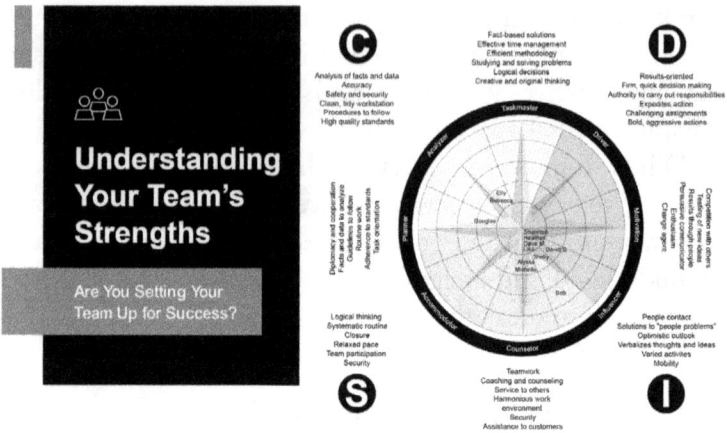

**Figure 3.1: Team Map Example**

This team's experience is not unique. Leaders often recreate themselves in the people they choose to hire and promote, even unintentionally. Over time, this unconscious bias can shape entire organizations.

Research from Korn Ferry shows that diverse teams make better decisions 87 percent of the time. Eighty percent of the most admired companies in the world create diverse teams to improve performance, creativity, and innovation. All too often, team members jump in to handle day-to-day tasks without truly understanding each other's strengths. Only when we fully understand each other's strengths can we fully support one another. Examples often come up when coaching teams, and when I initially engage, one of the first steps is to perform a diagnostic in which I create a team map I can walk through with the entire team to gain clarity.

## From Difference to Collective Insight

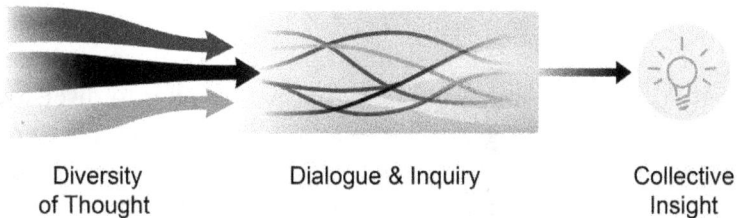

| Diversity of Thought | Dialogue & Inquiry | Collective Insight |

**Figure 3.2: Transition to Collective insight**

## The Risks of Homogeneous Teams

When teams lack diversity of thought and experience, three predictable problems emerge:

### Echo Chambers

Everyone agrees with each other. Ideas are recycled, and innovative thinking evaporates.

### Skill Gaps

Important capabilities—like driving execution or challenging assumptions—are neglected because no one feels comfortable stepping outside the group consensus.

### Stagnation

Over time, the team loses the agility to adapt. Performance plateaus or declines.

The evidence is clear. Deloitte's research showed that inclusive teams outperform their peers by **80 percent in team-based assessments**.[10] Korn Ferry found that diverse teams make better decisions nearly **9 out of 10 times**.[11]

Diversity isn't a philosophical ideal. It's a strategic advantage. What is often left out is that, when we refer to diversity, it is not just about gender or race. We all have had different experiences in our lives. I grew up in a home where we did not have much, as my father enlisted in the military at a young age and then worked as a draftsman for a factory in Cleveland. We lived below paycheck to paycheck. Every May, we picked out three sets of school clothes and put them on layaway so we could pay them off by September. The mall was just for rich kids.

I tell this story because it shaped my behavior and personality. When referring to the DISC assessment, I score a 99 out of 100 on the D (Dominance) Scale, meaning I want to get stuff done. If you didn't show up at 5 p.m. sharp for dinner because your basketball coach kept you late at practice, you didn't eat that evening. Not saying that is a way to raise kids. It simply emphasizes that I, as a leader, brought those attributes to the workplace, where being on time meant arriving at least five minutes early.

It is time to appreciate and celebrate the differences team members bring to the workplace. When teams are diverse, they bring new ideas and perspectives, creating an environment where innovation can thrive. If you attend most industry conferences today, you'll hear keynote speakers proclaiming the importance of diversity and inclusion. They cite data and reference compelling business cases. And yet, when you examine the numbers over time, progress is excruciatingly slow.

Consider the wealth management field. In 2010, according to Zippia, nearly **69 percent of advisors were men**, and over **78 percent were white**.[12] After a decade of initiatives—training programs, recruitment incentives, public commitments to change—those numbers barely budged. By 2021, the male proportion was still over 69 percent, and the percentage of white advisors had declined by less than 7 percent. This pattern isn't unique to financial services. A landmark CECP study on corporate social engagement found that while companies publicly emphasize diversity and inclusion, most struggle to translate those commitments into measurable, sustained progress.[13] This gap between intention and execution reinforces why leaders must do the internal work to understand their biases and actively build environments where true diversity of thought can thrive.

The story is similar in technology. Despite decades of awareness campaigns, only **26 percent of computing jobs are held by women,** and **just 3 percent are held by African American women.**[14] These statistics aren't just data points; they are proof that good intentions are not enough. Leaders must examine their own preferences, beliefs, and blind spots if they hope to change outcomes.

## The Three Commitments: Building a Foundation for Diversity of Thought

When teams struggle to collaborate effectively, I encourage them to adopt **Three Commitments.** These are not one-time activities as they are intended to be daily practices:

### Know Thyself

Each person reflects on their strengths, growth opportunities, and natural tendencies. This requires vulnerability and self-awareness.

## Appreciation

Team members commit to valuing different styles, even when those styles feel uncomfortable or unfamiliar.

## Be Curious

Instead of assuming motives or dismissing perspectives, the team leans into questions. Curiosity creates the space where innovation grows.

These commitments are the foundation of every high-performing, inclusive team I've seen.

One thing I emphasize is that the three commitments are not meant to be a one-and-done conversation. They are meant to be an ongoing discussion and a foundation for the team to build on. Much like a house, if you have a crumbling foundation, then the rest of the structure will eventually fall.

Keep that foundation strong by revisiting the three commitments regularly as a team. We have all been to an off-site team meeting, conference, or virtual seminar where we might have learned a few things, incorporated them for a week, and then slid back into our old habits. Don't allow this to happen. Remember, when we started this case study, the leader was having difficulty with the stated quantitative goals and did not mention any qualitative measures the team was using.

After I present the three commitments to the team, I provide coaching sessions where I take time to review the traits associated with each team member's personality style. This is the fun part because it allows us to assign roles that fit each player's natural tendencies, which usually sparks curiosity and excitement. In a team setting, everyone can hear about their team members' strengths, personality styles, and how they support success for the overall team.

Typically, in these situations, coaches hold one-on-one meetings with team members; however, I choose to hold these discussions as a team for a few reasons. I would challenge you and your team to take a similar approach, as it can accelerate trust and appreciation, and allow the authenticity we have been focused on to elevate within the team when everyone can hear about their team members.

Reasons to have these discussions as a team:

- The entire team hears the same message together as they work on these skills, rather than second-hand, where, as we all know, things can get lost in translation.
- Each team member can engage and discuss how they feel about the results. They can ask their teammates questions to increase their understanding. (This is where ownership and accountability are driven from, rather than being dictated to.) It allows each team member to be involved and contribute throughout the entire process.
- These discussions will equip the team with the skills to develop a team contract that outlines their future engagement with each other. Trust, healthy debate, what they will measure, and how they will hold each other accountable are a few topics that can be annotated in the contract. (We will discuss how to build this out in the next chapter, so stay tuned!)

## The Overall Goal

Our goal is to build an optimally performing team where everyone feels understood and appreciated, which will support authenticity within the team. While it's nice for leaders to share this message in team meetings, conferences, and off-sites, it should never stop there. Leaders and team members need to make sure the conversations continue and that everyone feels they have permission to show up with their uniqueness shining through, knowing they are supported. There needs to be freedom to hold healthy debates, have conversations with substance, and share their unique knowledge. With hybrid and remote positions now the workplace norm, it's more critical than ever to create an environment that prioritizes effective communication and knowledge sharing.

When speaking with leaders and their teams, I often challenge them to think about the lack of different viewpoints shared. This is ultimately the cause of bias and the reason many employees just nod along with what the leader says. So, what causes this? Is it the leader's resistance to hiring someone who thinks differently from them? Could it be fear that someone from a different background may not be able to contribute at a high enough level?

It is time for the message to meet the results when it comes to creating diverse teams. Whether you are a leader in the C-Suite, are managing your first team, or are a member of a team that lacks appreciation for each other's differences, I want to challenge you to take on this responsibility. To do this, you will need to develop a game plan.

## Case Study: The Telecom Team and the Crisis That Built Trust

In early 2020, a telecom company I supported faced unprecedented challenges. Their infrastructure powered hospitals, universities, and government facilities. As COVID-19 lockdowns spread, demand surged the team rallied in a way that inspired me. Long hours, tight deadlines, and constant uncertainty created an environment where everyone stepped up. They made decisions quickly and trusted each other implicitly. But when the crisis subsided, something shifted. The urgency disappeared. Meetings grew tense. Turnover spiked. Deadlines slipped.

The thoughtful executive leader, I'll call Greg, was baffled. "We were closer than ever during COVID," he said. "But now it feels like everyone is working against each other." I asked Greg to consider a question: "What did your team gain during the crisis that you haven't sustained?" After some reflection, he said, "Clarity and trust. Everyone knew their role and how much we depended on each other."

That was the insight he needed. The crisis had forced them to embrace vulnerability, urgency, and shared purpose. But once the adrenaline faded, they drifted back into old habits by defaulting to silos, avoiding tough conversations, and assuming alignment without verifying it. This was a highly matrixed organization, and the understanding of the diversity of thought and experience that assisted them in executing through urgency had now fallen by the wayside.

In my experience as a coach, "A-ha" moments are everything. There is nothing like seeing a team that is involved and appreciative of one another, aware of the different skills they bring to the table. It allows team members to understand each other's abilities, where everyone feels permission to be their authentic selves when they face challenges together.

Everyone brings unique viewpoints, perspectives, and knowledge. The beauty lies in sharing these unique traits, with the entire team benefiting and consistently performing at an optimal level. If you are a fan of the show *Ted Lasso*, then you will understand what a Coach Beard moment is. I've been fortunate enough to watch teams react as their natural strengths are mapped out together, providing open, objective data that sparks curiosity about their strengths. In quite a few instances, both leaders and their team members have had their Coach Beard moment, the quirky assistant coach to the infamous Ted Lasso known for his outbursts during meetings as if he is meaning to use his inside voice with his loud gasp or nervous laugh let out in the back of the room which can bring a laugh or levity to the situation although leads to confusion as well as discomfort among some team members.

## Tactics for Building a Diverse and Empowered Team

You may be wondering, "So what do I do about this?" Here are practical steps to move beyond good intentions:

### 1. Map Your Team

Use an assessment like DISC, StrengthsFinder, or Hogan to visualize where your team naturally clusters. Don't rely on guesswork; make the data visible and hold conversations about how each team member can contribute to projects and tasks, and about strengths that might not be part of your repertoire. In Michelle's team, seeing the map made the similarity effect undeniable. For Dave, it clarified that his team lacked drivers who could move initiatives forward.

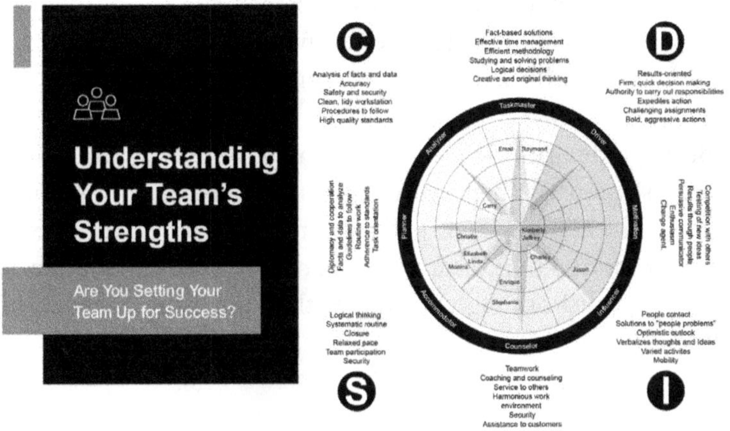

**Figure 3.3: Team Map Example**

## 2. Facilitate Strengths Conversations

Create space for each team member to share two or three strengths and a few growth areas. Model this vulnerability yourself. When leaders go first, they set the tone for openness. When Tom and I coach teams, we have witnessed firsthand how this step alone can shift a team's culture. When people hear their colleagues speak candidly about what they bring to the table in terms of their strengths, passions, and what they're still working on, it humanizes everyone and brings the team closer together.

## 3. Design a Team Contract

A team contract is a written agreement that defines how you will collaborate, debate, and make decisions. It addresses questions like:

How will we handle disagreements?
How will we balance efficiency and inclusion?
How will we hold each other accountable?

I often guide teams in co-creating these contracts during facilitated sessions. When everyone contributes, buy-in is much higher, as empowerment and ownership become part of your organization's DNA. You allow team members to help create how you will work together, rather than imposing a dictatorial approach.

### 4. Review Regularly

Once you have a contract, don't let it collect dust. Revisit it quarterly. Ask: Are we honoring our commitments? What's working? What needs to evolve?

## Team Map Aligned to Natural Strengths

When it comes time to review the team map, here are a few things to keep in mind:

1. First, we want to be open and objective. Each team member needs to review this data to understand everyone's strengths. From there, they'll be able to see how everyone plays a role in executing the vision and mission, and how they can support the organization's success in achieving its goals.
2. The team will likely see gaps in overall natural strengths and roles. This is fine, as it raises awareness of what is currently available in terms of the team's strengths, as well as our third commitment . . . **Be Curious.**
3. Lastly, this team map is not intended to give the leader a reason to fire team members who might be too much

like other team members and hire others to fill in the gaps. This is about awareness and authenticity together as a cohesive team, so that strengths and opportunities for improvement are prioritized.

## Case Study: The Telecom Team's Renewal

Returning to the telecom team, Greg and I embarked on this process. We started by mapping the team's DISC profiles. It quickly became clear that decision-making and follow-through were underrepresented. People were engaged but were hesitant to assert ideas that might create tension.

Over the next six months, Greg held monthly reflection sessions. The team designed a contract outlining how they'd communicate and hold each other accountable. They adopted the Three Commitments as a standing agenda item, with each meeting starting with a quick check-in on how they were practicing self-awareness, appreciation, and curiosity.

The results were striking. Turnover decreased, project timelines improved, and the team reported feeling more connected. As Greg put it, "We stopped relying on crisis to make us a team."

## Reflection Questions

To help you assess your team, consider these questions:

- When was the last time someone disagreed with me in a meeting?
- How do I react when that happens?
- What is the composition of my team's strengths and styles?
- How have I contributed—intentionally or unintentionally—to our culture?

- Which of the Three Commitments am I modeling consistently?
- Which do I avoid or overlook?

## Your Next Steps

If you want to create an environment where diversity of thought thrives, Tom and I invite you to take these steps.

### Inventory Your Team

Complete an assessment to understand your team's natural styles, strengths, and gaps. Have conversations about everyone's strengths and discuss together how you can work more effectively as a team.

### Invite Candid Conversations

Schedule time for each person to share their perspectives. Don't rush this foundational step. The homework inquiry we have team members complete in this section is to hold one-on-one conversations with each team member and be intentional with the time. Share two to three personal strengths to bring awareness to everyone on the team so that there is clarity and understanding on how you can contribute your skills further to accomplishing the goals of the team and how your team members can lean on you in the future. Lastly, share two to three opportunities that you want to focus on improving. This will continue to enhance vulnerability and humility on the team.

### Implement the Three Commitments

Make self-awareness, appreciation, and curiosity explicit expectations. Once again, do not make these conversations "check the box" moments. Create a culture where team members feel that they are contributing to the organization's goals. Make sure they feel that their unique skills are valued and appreciated.

## Invest in Ongoing Learning

Block time to revisit your team contract and adjust as your team evolves. This is where alignment can take hold of your team: understanding how to communicate effectively with one another and build additional rapport, while recognizing that differences can contribute to the team excelling in the future. Research shows that diverse teams that contribute different strengths and viewpoints outperform teams that lack this insight.[15]

## Conclusion: From Ordinary to Extraordinary

When you champion diversity of thought, experience, and perspective, you elevate your team from ordinary to extraordinary. You build a culture where people feel safe to be themselves—and inspired to contribute their best ideas.

It's tempting to believe that trust and inclusion are soft skills that emerge organically, but in reality, they result from deliberate practice, honest reflection, and courageous leadership.

The teams that outperform their peers are not the ones with the most polished mission statements. They are the ones where leaders do the daily work of creating an environment where everyone's uniqueness is celebrated and harnessed for the good of the whole. It happens when team members can feel that they can bring their authentic selves to the workplace and fulfill the responsibilities of their roles. It's when leaders can build a culture where differences are seen as a welcome part of how their teams collaborate and innovate.

Creating an environment where authenticity can thrive and is encouraged can separate your team from being ordinary to reaching the full potential of the collective group, and, as shown in the research, support your team in being extraordinary in meeting or exceeding results.

## Leader Self-Assessment: Inclusive Leadership Readiness

Rate each statement from 1 (Strongly Disagree) to 5 (Strongly Agree).

1. I actively seek out diverse perspectives when making decisions.
2. I am aware of my own unconscious biases.
3. I model vulnerability by sharing my growth areas with my team.
4. I create space for team members to discuss their strengths and differences.
5. I regularly review the composition and skill gaps in my team.
6. I encourage healthy debate and do not penalize dissent.
7. I reinforce our commitments to curiosity, appreciation, and self-awareness.
8. I integrate diversity and inclusion into our performance metrics.
9. I invest time in developing inclusive practices.
10. I celebrate successes that result from leveraging diverse thinking.

## Taking Action

- Spend time together understanding the team's strengths and, in individual meetings, have each team member share two to three strengths they bring to the team from their perspective, for 30 minutes.
- Discuss how, as a team, we can grow an appreciation for our differences and prioritize learning about each team member's unique traits and experiences.
- Hold a team meeting to discuss at least three commitments the team can make so that, when we are innovating, collaborating, or working on projects, we can consider including team members with diverse thoughts and experiences.
- Discuss how the team can show up and be curious for each other so that individuals can let go of their judgment or personal biases when they appear.
- Create two to three action steps the team can take to gain appreciation for each other's strengths and how they can be applied in the future.

# CHAPTER 4

## Seeing Each Other Clearly: Creating Synergy on Your Team

*When awareness is brought to an emotion,*
*power is brought to your life.*
—Tara Meyer Robson

## Why Synergy Requires Awareness

When leaders talk about creating a high-performing team, they often focus on strategy, planning, and execution. Those elements matter, but they miss the essential foundation: awareness of the people involved. Teams thrive when every individual feels seen, respected, and understood. Without this, collaboration remains surface-level.

Tom and I have coached countless teams that believed they were aligned until we started exploring the ways they misunderstood one another. They thought the lack of progress was about skills or knowledge gaps. More often, it was simply a lack of curiosity about each other's preferences, strengths, and emotional needs. Think about the best teams you've been part of, either at work, in sports, or even in your family. It wasn't just that you shared a common goal. You trusted one another enough to share ideas and challenge each other without fear. That is the heart of synergy: psychological safety anchored in mutual awareness.

## Formula 1 Teams: Synchronized Synergy

Tom and I are coaching and research geeks. We both wear the title like a badge of honor, so we are always looking at teams' performance in Fortune 500 organizations, small businesses, non-profits, and sports organizations. When you watch a Formula 1 race, it's easy to get captivated by the driver whom many recognize as the lone figure in the cockpit, maneuvering a car at 200 miles per hour. But behind every driver is a team of hundreds, all committed to the same mission: delivering world-class performance in the most competitive environment imaginable.

In many ways, Formula 1 is a laboratory for creating teams that operate at an optimal level of performance. It's a place where preparation, clarity, and trust converge, and where even the smallest breakdown in alignment can lead to failure. The larger teams, such as Mercedes, Red Bull, and Ferrari, can have as many as 1,200 team members. They all need to understand their roles, respect each other's ideas, and work as a collective to focus on one thing: the team winning.

During a pit stop, twenty crew members complete an intricate choreography in less than three seconds. Tires are changed, fuel is measured, and adjustments are made. Each person knows exactly where to stand, what to do, and when to move. If even one person hesitates or deviates, the entire race can be lost. That level of coordination requires extreme clarity of roles and responsibilities, something most business teams struggle to achieve.

Formula 1 teams rely on real-time data and constant feed-back. Sensors in the car transmit thousands of data points every second, enabling the pit wall to adjust strategy on the fly. The drivers receive information about tire degradation, fuel load, and competitor behavior, all while racing at the edge of human capability. In business, feedback is often delayed or sugarcoated. Feedback must be immediate and honest.

Perhaps the most striking aspect of Formula 1 is the trust between driver and team. When a driver pits at 200 mph, he is trusting dozens of people to execute flawlessly. When the team radios a change in strategy, the driver must trust the team's judgment without hesitation.

This level of trust doesn't happen by accident. It's built through repetition, transparency, and shared commitment to excellence.

## Preparation Makes the Extraordinary Look Routine

From the outside, a perfect pit stop looks effortless. But behind the scenes, teams have practiced that stop thousands of times. They analyze every motion, every possible contingency, every detail. Preparation is what makes excellence look easy.

In leadership, the same principle applies: the more intentional you are about planning and rehearsing, the more graceful your performance under pressure. This includes setting the expectation for effective communication and understanding the collective's strengths. When Tom and I see teams struggle, in most cases, qualitative competencies are inhibiting them from reaching the level of success they seek.

You can tell we are fascinated by Formula 1. The point of the story here is that it is time to take a stand. It is time to focus on respecting and understanding your team members' differences so the collective can reach its potential.

In this chapter, we will focus on how you can increase your team members' ability to bring their authentic selves to the roles they play. On a Formula 1 team, whether in the role of a race engineer, data analyst, mechanic, or pit crew member, everyone needs to be in sync and appreciate what each member brings to the team. They need to bring their authentic selves to be fully energized and in tune with how they contribute, which we will discuss throughout this chapter.

## The Hidden Cost of Judging Differences

When team members don't understand each other's wiring, they start to make assumptions. We all know the colleague who questions every proposal. Over time, others label them as difficult or negative, or the person who rarely speaks in meetings gets categorized as disengaged. What if these interpretations are simply misunderstandings?

One nonprofit board I supported provides a powerful example. The Executive Director, Mindy, was working with eight board members, most of whom were from Fortune 500 companies. They cared deeply about the mission, but donations were lagging. Mindy told me she hesitated to address the fundraising shortfall. "I'm worried they'll think I'm criticizing them," she admitted. "We don't have that kind of relationship."

This was a board full of smart, well-meaning people. However, without trust and understanding, the fear of conflict outweighed the desire to improve. So, they kept showing up to quarterly meetings, politely avoiding the conversation everyone knew they needed to have. Tom and I have seen this same dynamic in teams across industries that we have coached: fear of tension keeps problems hidden. Over time, the cost is stagnation, frustration, and missed opportunities.

## From Misinterpretation to Shared Meaning

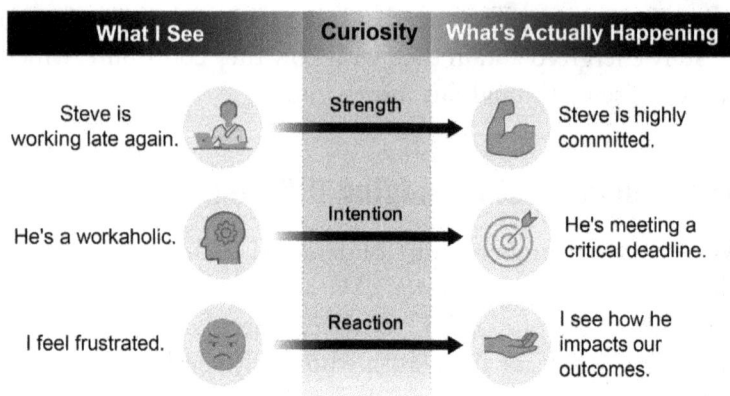

| What I See | Curiosity | What's Actually Happening |
|---|---|---|
| Steve is working late again. | Strength | Steve is highly committed. |
| He's a workaholic. | Intention | He's meeting a critical deadline. |
| I feel frustrated. | Reaction | I see how he impacts our outcomes. |

Figure 4.1: Creating Shared Meaning on a Team

# The Power of Knowing Yourself First

Awareness begins with understanding your own patterns. We all carry stories that shape how we work and what we believe is acceptable, safe, or effective. Personally, I've had this conversation with my spouse of almost 30 years, as we both came from different experiences.

I grew up in a Cleveland, Ohio, household that was about as blue-collar as it gets. I moved to Southern California to attend college, where I met a surfer girl from the area, and the rest is history. We have two boys, and I remember when the oldest was turning 16, my spouse asked what type of car we were going to buy him. Buy him? In my house, the most you could count on is possibly a co-signature, so you could get a loan and pay your own expenses.

I prided myself on working hard to make my own way, with decisiveness and efficiency. Although for a long time, I didn't realize how that came across to others, especially my wife, who needed more time to process and was stunned that someone had to work while in high school.

I'm a High D on the DISC profile, affectionately referred to as a dominant, action-oriented, results-focused individual. In many ways, this trait has been an asset. However, I had to learn that my natural style could overwhelm team members who valued stability over speed. When I finally recognized this, I stopped expecting everyone to adapt to my way of thinking. I learned to flex my approach and ask more questions. That shift transformed my relationships with colleagues, clients, and my wonderful wife, who, in the end, won, being able to "hand down" cars to the boys and purchase a new one for herself when appropriate. What can I say, she has a high Influencing style.

## Understanding and Appreciating Different Personalities

When Tom and I engage with a team, we often use a personality assessment so team members can develop self-awareness of their personality styles and understand their similarities and differences. The DISC framework is the one we will use most often to help teams gain this level of self-awareness. It's not a magic solution, but it is a powerful starting point.

Here's a clear overview:

### Dominance (D)

Strengths: Decisive, direct, confident.
Needs: Autonomy, fast results.
Struggles: Impatience, tendency to dominate conversations.

## Influence (I)

Strengths: Inspiring, enthusiastic, collaborative.
Needs: Social connection, recognition.
Struggles: Distraction, glossing over details.

**The DISC Model**

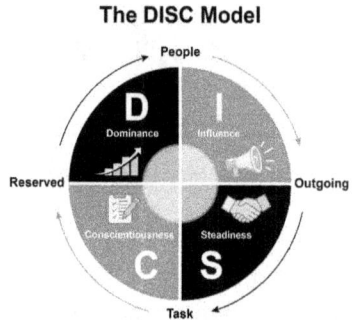

## Steadiness (S)

Strengths: Dependable, patient, empathetic.
Needs: Stability, clarity.
Struggles: Avoiding change, hesitating to assert opinions.

**Figure 4.2: The DISC Model**

## Conscientiousness (C)

Strengths: Analytical, precise, careful.
Needs: Clear standards, accuracy.
Struggles: Overthinking, difficulty delegating

When people understand these patterns, they stop taking differences personally. They see them as assets to harness rather than obstacles to manage.

## The Driver (High D Personality)

- Need for control
- Fear of helplessness
- Struggles with telling

When focusing first on dominance (D), we discussed how it measures how they approach problems and challenges. I cannot count the number of times an employee who tested as a high D immediately thought they were considered a dominant individual in every aspect of their life. It's understandably confusing, but the key is that the assessment can be scored on a 1–100 scale for each personality style and reflects what gives an individual energy, both in their natural and adapted strengths.

Personally, this is my highest measured trait, where I score 99 out of 100 in how I approach problems and challenges. As a High D, the words that describe my approach are control, authority, challenge, and influence. I get energy from coming up with new ideas, and competition can take over from time to time, as I want our team to win.

However, without awareness, this can show up as overpowering or even aggressive to team members, as I can get passionate about innovating processes or procedures to elevate our overall performance. This was a big "a-ha" moment for me as a leader because I had developed these traits through my personal experience growing up. (If you catch me at a conference, you can pull me aside and provide me with a free therapy session!)

## Social (High I Personality)

- Need for attention
- Fear of insignificance
- Struggles with listening

Influence (I) measures how you engage with others. Do you seek out interactions with people, or are you more private? Remember, this assessment measures what gives you energy, so if an employee is above the line with their natural strengths, they enjoy influencing others and are more social, outgoing, and optimistic. If they are below the line, they prefer more privacy and take longer to develop relationships because they are more cautious, relying on facts, information, and logic.

In some instances, you may notice that an employee is a natural high I, while they are an adapted low I. There can be several reasons for this shift, but typically it means they are adapting their style to meet what they feel their role calls for to be successful. In my C-Suite team, one leader felt they couldn't speak up during team meetings and other conversations, so they shifted their natural strength down to adopt a more cautious approach.

Without awareness of this, the leader could experience burnout or emotions such as anxiety or frustration, all so they can perform in line with expectations. But how long would they be able to go on like that? Some team members may be able to maintain this level of frustration for the next few years, but if they don't effectively communicate their personality type, it could lead to internal as well as external conflict in the future.

Remember, everyone is unique, so there is no set time that someone could operate in a role that doesn't align well with their natural strengths. For that reason, it is important to check in and establish a game plan to prevent the burnout or even boredom that can set in if their current role is not fueling their energy.

## The Empathizer (High S Personality)

- Need for approval
- Fear of rejection
- Struggles with closing

Steadiness (S) involves measuring the pace of your environment. If you score above the energy line, you value a stable, structured, and predictable environment, where time is needed in advance to address changes within the organization. Results that fall below the energy line indicate someone who welcomes and thrives on change, seeking a fast-paced environment with variety.

A lack of awareness can lead to frustration at the individual level and cause team members to disengage from you. An individual on the team with a high S is described as reliable, systematic, thorough, and consistent, while a low S is described as flexible, active, unattached, and adaptable. I've witnessed many teams where conflict is prevalent because team members lack understanding and appreciation.

Imagine how you could support a team member who might be the opposite of you when it comes to steadiness. If you need time to adjust to change, and some team members have this as a strength, what would it do for the team to lean into one another when anticipating the need for a new process, procedure, or shift in responsibilities? How might the team operate more quickly through change if team members could be open about their need for support?

## The Analyzer (High C Personality)

- Need for information
- Fear of being wrong
- Struggles with relating

The last personality style is conscientiousness (C), which measures your connection to rules and procedures. A high C will be described as more detail-oriented, analytical, and driven to follow rules and systems to minimize errors. A low C values independence and wants to establish their own rules. I always say that the low C will be the one whose mantra can be, "If it's not broken, let's break it so we can figure out a better way."

Once again, I want you to notice how the differences between the high and low ends of individual assessment results can lead to ineffective communication and/or conflict within a team. If the team has a high concentration of individuals with a high C trait, how might that pull the team back from making quick decisions? What would it look like to have awareness and build synergy together by understanding how to support each other through your different strengths? In most cases, these differences go unnoticed, creating obstacles for teams and creating unwanted drag on the implementation and execution of ideas.

Over the past decade, I have analyzed a team's dynamics and almost feel like a mind reader, knowing they probably have projects they've considered but haven't implemented. Their fear of failure makes them think things must be perfect, so they need more and more data.

When many different approaches are paired with a lack of empathy, they can result in limited team success. Therefore, Tom and I both stress the importance of knowing thyself before moving forward to focus on the team. Having awareness of who *you* are and how *you* operate can give you confidence and empower you to contribute more effectively to the team environment. Building team cohesion starts with becoming aware of your strengths and opportunities for improvement, leading you to show up for team conversations with courage, humility, and appreciation for the growth you've achieved.

## Case Study: The C-Suite Team Map

One of the most transformative engagements I facilitated was with an 18-member executive team at a financial services firm. The CEO, Dave, was a classic High D/I, energized by change and always in motion. The rest of his leadership team leaned heavily toward High S and High C. They valued predictability, thoroughness, and clear protocols.

At first, they thought their challenges were purely operational. They weren't meeting key performance indicators, and projects were falling behind. When we assessed their DISC profiles and mapped them visually, the picture came into focus.

Their natural styles created tension. Dave pushed for rapid decisions. His team wanted time to analyze and plan. Each side assumed the other was being difficult. In reality, they were simply expressing their instincts, without recognizing or appreciating their team members' different thoughts and ideas.

When we reviewed everyone's personality profile together, there was a quiet moment of recognition. One leader said, "I finally see why this feels so hard. We're all trying to do our best, but we have been speaking different languages." That insight laid the groundwork for more honest conversations. Dave asked, "How can I support you through this change?" Team members felt safer admitting when they needed more time or clarity. Over time, they moved from polite frustration to authentic collaboration as they began to recognize each other's differences and "flex" to the needs of the individual rather than a sort of "my way or the highway" approach.

## Appreciating Each Other's Uniqueness

Awareness isn't enough if it stays theoretical. Teams must practice appreciation so that everyone can actively recognize and value each person's contributions. One exercise I recommend is simple: have each team member share two things that energize them and two that drain them in the workplace. This often uncovers hidden truths and will be in your results, whether it is DISC, the Hogan Assessments, the Kolbe A™ Index, or another assessment of your choice.

In one session, a leader admitted, "I need time to think before I share ideas. When I'm pushed to decide in the moment, I shut down." Another said, "I thrive when I can bounce ideas around without worrying about whether they're perfect." These conversations build empathy. They remind us that people's reactions are usually about their needs and not about us. As I mentioned earlier, we all have unique experiences that shape our behavior. Usually, we are attracted to natural traits that are similar to our own. I won't go into detail here, but look up the Similarity Effect, and you will see that this has been heavily researched. When we can be curious together and allow ourselves to understand and appreciate our team members, it creates the synergy that most teams find eludes them.

Without awareness and appreciation for what makes each member unique, you can talk to your team all day long, but until you show them exactly what you are referring to, it might not click. Remember, we are not attempting to change anyone. Instead, we are highlighting differences in personality styles and approaches to help each team member feel appreciated. This method raises the potential of the individual and the team in a cohesive manner.

## The Role of Emotional Needs

Each DISC style has predictable emotional needs and fears:

### Table 4.1: Emotional Needs Matrix

| DISC Type | Core Needs | Core Fears |
|---|---|---|
| Dominance (D) | Autonomy, Achievement | Loss of Control |
| Influence (I) | Connection, Recognition | Rejection, Disconnection |
| Steadiness (S) | Stability, Clarity | Sudden Change, Instability |
| Conscientiousness (C) | Accuracy, Standards | Criticism, Being Wrong |

When those needs are threatened, people disengage or become defensive. This is where we, as team members, need to pay attention to which emotions may appear. For example, when different approaches are paired with a lack of empathy, it can result in limited team success. Therefore, Tom and I both stress the importance of knowing thyself before moving forward to focus on the team. Having awareness of who *you* are and how *you* operate can give you confidence and empower you to contribute more effectively to the team environment.

Understanding these needs and fears is another key to unlocking greatness within the team. Tom and I have both had this discussion with leaders and their teams about the roadblocks that can arise when team members are operating from personal needs. In addition, fears can drive behaviors. Bringing this forward so the team can have an open discussion allows everyone to rebuild appreciation. It is a driver of permitting individuals to be their authentic selves in the workplace.

Review the table above in an upcoming team meeting and discuss your needs and fears. Who on the team has a need for control, where their intentions on a recent project were well-intended but rubbed others the wrong way? What is happening when team members become silent during team meetings? How can you create an environment that places fear on the table so you can be curious about what might get in the way moving forward?

Tom and I teach that authenticity's foundation is creating a culture where these topics can be discussed openly rather than hidden. We are all human, and being able to discuss these emotions can provide a support system, especially when things go off track. Discuss your differences here and support each other when negative behaviors might appear. What steps will the team take to get back on track?

## Healthy Debate as a Core Competency

Patrick Lencioni has written extensively about the importance of "productive conflict."[16] In our experience coaching teams, we refer to it as "healthy debate," which seems to prevent negative emotions from escalating into conflict. It is one of the most underdeveloped skills on teams. People confuse disagreement with disrespect. They avoid tension, thinking it preserves harmony. But the opposite is true: avoided conflict becomes resentment.

We often ask teams, "What's your relationship with conflict?" In response, you'll see nervous glances, fidgeting, or laughter. It's a question that gets under the surface.

Healthy debate requires clear ground rules:

- Disagreement is not a personal attack.
- Questions are an expression of engagement.
- Different perspectives make us stronger.

Research on inspiring leadership shows that teams perform at higher levels when leaders model vulnerability, openness, and a willingness to engage in honest dialogue. Zenger and Folkman found that the most inspiring leaders create environments where people feel safe to challenge ideas and contribute fully as team members begin to feel empowered to explore what's possible.[17]

## Case Example: The Nonprofit Board Revisited

Remember Mindy's board? Once they committed to understanding each other, they shifted from polite meetings to productive dialogue. They acknowledged their discomfort with fundraising conversations. They admitted their fear of conflict. Gradually, they developed a shared language.

At their next quarterly meeting, Mindy opened with a simple statement: "I believe we all want this organization to thrive. Let's be honest about what's working and what's not." That invitation unlocked a wave of ideas, positive accountability, and collaboration. Six months later, their fundraising was ahead of target. Not because of a new strategy, but because they finally felt safe to challenge each other.

## The Synergy Leadership Loop

Figure 4.3: The Synergy Leadership Loop

## Your Next Steps

Creating synergy is a practice. It requires ongoing reflection, deliberate action, and a willingness to be uncomfortable. Make time to take the steps listed below and hold meaningful conversations with the members of your team, focused on the following:

1. Identify individual personalities on the team.
2. Talk about your differences.
3. Make space for healthy debate.
4. Revisit your agreements often.

When you do, you will discover that the uniqueness of each team member can be the source of your greatest strength.

## Conclusion: The Courage to See Each Other Clearly

Teams that outperform are rarely those with the most talent on paper. They are the ones who learn to see each other clearly without judgment and commit to working together as whole, complex human beings.

Awareness. Appreciation. Action. That's the path to synergy and to results you never imagined possible.

## Taking Action

- Know thyself by identifying the different personalities on the team and discussing needs and fears.
- Spend time learning about each other's strengths and communication styles, along with how you can work together more effectively in the future.
- Discuss team commitments that you can make together to recognize and appreciate your diversity of strengths and communication preferences so that we can collectively strive to reach high performance together.
- Describe a time that you were part of a team where you did not feel you could bring your natural strengths to your role. Discuss with your team members in your preferred setting.
- Envision the future by detailing what it would look like for the team to have awareness and appreciation for each other's abilities. How would this change the team's results, both qualitatively and quantitatively?

# CHAPTER 5

# Cultivating Ownership

*Act as if what you do makes a difference. It does.*
—William James

## Rethinking Ownership and Accountability

The words "accountability" and "ownership" are often tossed around in organizations as if simply saying them is enough, although in practice, they're among the most misunderstood and misused concepts in leadership. How many times have you heard, *"I'm going to hold you accountable,"* delivered like a threat? Most people associate accountability with stress and fear rather than empowerment. Contrast that with a different approach: *"How can we support you?"* or *"What will you do differently to succeed?"* Same intention, different impact.

When you shift the tone of accountability from blame to curiosity, you create the foundation for ownership. In this environment, team members don't simply comply; now they contribute. They don't wait for orders; they feel they are empowered to act.

A few years ago, I was coaching a leader of a large wealth management team. The business was struggling to hit growth targets. When I asked what he thought was causing the gap, he said: *"They just won't do what I tell them."* He believed success depended on getting rid of underperformers. In reality, he hadn't set clear expectations or invited his team into the process of problem-solving.

This leader, like many, assumed others should read his mind, duplicate his behaviors, and perform without context or support. When people failed, he defaulted to judgment instead of reflection. But here's the truth: If you want ownership, you can't demand it. You must create an environment that is safe enough to step up.

## The Ownership Mindset

Ownership starts with clarity. People must understand what success looks like and why it matters. That's not the full story, though, as it also requires something deeper: a sense that their work has meaning and that they have permission to make decisions and take action.

Picture a culture where accountability isn't punitive but positive. A place where leaders say, *"How will you hold yourself accountable, and how can I support you?"* Instead of fear, there's pride and motivation. When you transform accountability from a demand into an invitation, you empower people to bring their best selves. When you frame the demand as a question and follow up with an offer to support them, the entire message changes.

You are now giving your team members permission to utilize their strengths with the freedom to create, knowing they have you, their leader, to support them. You are no longer dictating; you are sharing in the process for the greater good of the team. In most cases, when an employee is presented with this option, they will feel more comfortable engaging and taking ownership. When you use this technique, your employees will go from feeling fearful and unmotivated to feeling proud and encouraged.

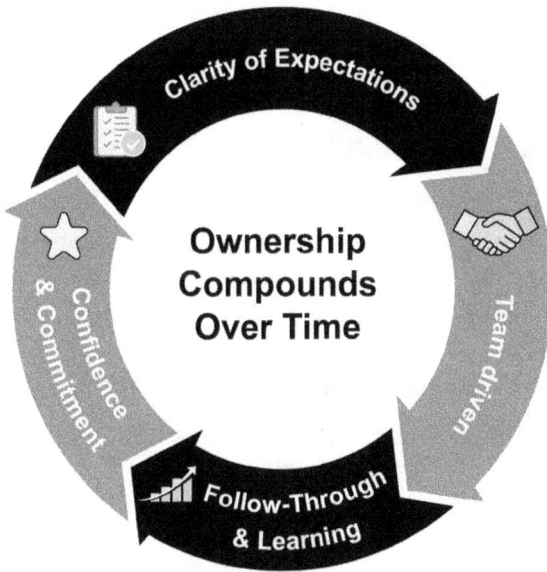

Figure 5.1: Path to Team Ownership

## Case Example: General McChrystal's Lesson

General Stanley McChrystal, author of *Team of Teams*, describes how he had to change his perspective when it came to empowering the members of his team during their time in Afghanistan.[18] McChrystal's fearless show of humility and vulnerability is admirable. In his book, he discusses instances when individuals would come knocking on his door at 3 a.m., asking for advice on simple decisions they had to make. If these soldiers had been empowered, there would have been no reason for them to seek help from McChrystal.

He realized that the problem wasn't their lack of initiative; it was the culture he'd allowed to develop. Without explicitly giving permission, he had inadvertently trained his team to rely on him for everything. His insight was simple but profound:

if you want people to own decisions, you must step back. You must replace control with trust.

## Challenge Your Beliefs

Now is the time to challenge your knowledge of accountability, empowerment, and ownership. It is time to create a culture where your team members commit to freeing the bottlenecks caused by your preconceived notions and beliefs. Forget about your past experiences and lean into what is possible.

In the following pages, Tom and I will dissect the concepts of accountability, empowerment, and ownership to create an environment where everyone is on the same page and can bring their authenticity to the team. We'll start by discussing the theory behind each concept, then we'll talk about how they can be used together to embolden a culture of ownership, which naturally leads to team cohesion. Take a moment to think about your team's current environment.

Ask yourself:

- How does the team define accountability?
- Do I believe it requires control?
- Do I feel safe letting others lead?

Ownership begins with leaders willing to release their grip.

## Positive Accountability

In *The Wisdom of Teams*, Douglas Smith and Jon Katzenbach describe mutual accountability as a defining attribute of high-performance teams.[19] However, accountability only works when it's anchored in respect, not fear. Tom and I have witnessed the damage caused by an authoritarian approach. Early in my own personal career as a leader, I was driven by a singular obsession with winning. If I could work sixteen hours, I expected everyone else to match me. If I met a goal, I assumed others would follow.

The key is to create accountability without triggering stress, and that comes down to how leaders set the tone. A lot of people may associate the word accountable with fear, frustration, and even anxiety. If they don't follow through with the task they are being held accountable for, they can naturally fear punishment.

That's not really a mindset that fosters team growth. Today, while I'm fully recovered from competing, I still find myself getting triggered by past experiences when the topic of accountability comes up. I always pause and have the team unpack what they are looking to achieve, so they can celebrate accountability rather than fear it. Looking back, I realize I created an environment where people were afraid to admit challenges. They complied outwardly but disengaged emotionally.

Over time, I learned a better way: **positive accountability.** It's built on three steps.

## Step 1: Establish the Right Mindset

First, explore how your team experiences accountability. Some people grew up in households where accountability meant punishment. Others were taught to equate accountability with failure. As we've discovered, it can be hard to establish accountability as a positive within the culture, which is why leaders often struggle with this first step. But I assure you, it is possible.

All it takes is a little communication and consistency. The first step for you, as the leader, is to let go of your judgment and spearhead conversations about accountability with the team. I caution you to approach this with curiosity.

Ask your team:

- How do we currently view accountability?
- What does it mean to us?
- How do we want it to feel in this culture?

James Clear, author of *Atomic Habits*, said, "I try to keep a mindset of baseline optimism." That mindset applies here. Approach these conversations with curiosity and empathy, not judgment. This is a challenge I would give to you, as a team member or leader, on how to approach these conversations, as there will be differences in opinions, once again based on each team member's unique relationship with accountability.

Capture the team's thoughts and commitments.

## Step 2: Define the Standard Together

Now, it's time to activate. After the team has had an open and honest conversation, with a promise to continue these conversations, it's time to create behaviors that everyone can follow. Much like in your personal life, the team will set standards for how to live and support one another in the day-to-day operations of the workplace, creating positive accountability.

If an individual is not meeting their goals, their teammates have permission to reach out and support them. Remember that messaging is critical in communication. How you relay this support will make or break the team's perspective of accountability.

Instead of burying your question beneath scrutiny and asking, "What's wrong with you? Why are you failing to meet deadlines?" shift the exchange to: "How can we support you?

What adjustments do you need to make to overcome any obstacles?"

Remember my competitive streak? In the past, I would've been the one to ask, "What's wrong with them?" I cringe just thinking about it. Now, after years spent working on my mindset, I have a very different approach, one that moves far from a message that creates negative feelings. Once you understand perceptions, co-create standards.

Invite everyone to articulate their commitments to supporting each other.

Use these questions:

- How will we communicate when someone falls behind?
- What language signals support instead of blame?
- What guardrails will help us reset when negativity creeps in?

In one team I coached, leaders replaced "*Why aren't you meeting expectations?*" with "*How can we help you get there?*" That simple change transformed the tone.

## Step 3: Review and Flex

Positive accountability is about supporting each other so the team can drive results for the organization. In addition, it is imperative to set expectations and co-create what accountability means together so that everyone on the team understands what it means to truly be accountable to one another. Again, establishing a new mindset and behaviors to support success in any area takes time, as we push beyond our old habits and create new ones that will accelerate our performance. You will need to make sure there is sufficient time for this last step.

Our day-to-day can be hectic, and if conversations are qualitative and hard to measure, they can take a back seat because we don't keep them top of mind. New habits fade without reinforcement. Schedule time quarterly to review your commitments.

Ask:

- Are we living up to our agreements?
- Where have we drifted?
- What do we need to adjust?

When accountability is woven into daily conversations, it becomes a shared value rather than a top-down directive.

## Empowerment: Moving Beyond Delegation

A leader once told me, *"I have to lead every project because nobody can execute the way I can."*

Sound familiar? Many leaders confuse delegation and empowerment. Delegation is assigning tasks. Empowerment is giving people ownership and authority. **Delegation is transactional. Empowerment is transformational.** If you only delegate, you get compliance. If you empower, you get commitment.

Empowerment is a crucial element, so you will need to consider it from a couple of different angles. First, as a leader, what do you need to raise your level of awareness and abilities to consistently empower your team members? I've heard a variety of different answers to this question.

> *I need to let go of my need for control.*
> *I'm not sure what steps I need to take to empower my team members.*
> *If I want to get something done right, I need to do it myself.*

Oxford defines empowerment as:

- *Authority or power given to someone to do something.*
- *The process of becoming stronger and more confident.*

Empowerment is not about abdicating responsibility. It's about creating conditions in which people can stretch toward their potential.

Do you feel that the first bullet point defines your approach? Maybe you attempt to delegate a few items every now and then, but you don't explain why or what success looks like to you.

Or does the second resonate with you more? Do you feel that the more you empower your team members to take on additional responsibilities, the more confident, comfortable, and in control they will feel of the impact they have on the organization's results? Think about how this would enhance your team members' authenticity, helping them feel more in control of their day-to-day, feel that what they do matters, and understand the impact their contributions have on the overall bottom line.

## Case Example: Mark's Transformation

Patrick, a senior leader I coached, struggled to empower his team. He tried to delegate, but when results fell short, he would take back control. Over time, we uncovered the root cause: Patrick didn't trust that delegation would succeed because he'd never been taught how to empower others. He thought giving tasks without context or support was enough.

Mark was confused about the differences between delegation and empowerment. Delegation is the process of distributing and entrusting work to another person, and it involves a task. Empowerment is giving *someone else* the power and authority. As a leader, your job is to do both: define what success will look like and instill confidence in your employees' abilities to execute, while providing support along the way.

One of my favorite quotes comes from marketer turned author Simon Sinek: "A star wants to see themselves rise to the top. A leader wants to see those around them rise to the top." One way to set your team up for success is to define delegation and empowerment so everyone has clarity about what you are trying to accomplish.

Once team members are on the same page as you, they will appreciate delegation because it will make them feel valued as they contribute to the organization's goals. According to a survey conducted by Stanford University, 35 percent of CEOs acknowledged that they need to strengthen their delegation skills, while 37 percent stated they are actively striving to enhance their delegation skills.[20]

When Mark learned to pair clear expectations with encouragement, everything changed. His team grew more confident. He discovered the freedom that comes when others are invested.

## The Five Characteristics of Empowerment

Through his research, author Hieu Minh Vu identified five characteristics that foster successful team empowerment:

- A sense of competence
- A sense of self-organization
- A sense of effectiveness
- A sense of meaningful contribution
- A sense of trust in others[21]

## The Five Characteristics of Empowerment

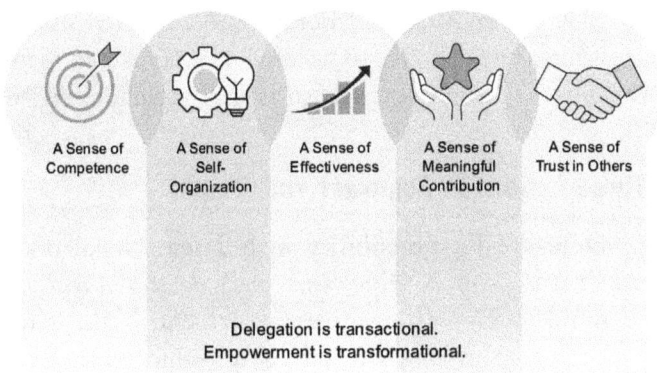

| A Sense of Competence | A Sense of Self-Organization | A Sense of Effectiveness | A Sense of Meaningful Contribution | A Sense of Trust in Others |

Delegation is transactional.
Empowerment is transformational.

**Figure 5.2: The 5 Characteristics of Empowerment**

When these conditions exist, people step up without being asked. Empowerment is much more than handling someone else's tasks. It is a culture and environment where team members feel connected to a purpose, with a sense of pride and achievement as they contribute to something bigger than themselves. This is where they feel valued, given the opportunity to continually develop and contribute to the team in more meaningful ways beyond daily tasks. In addition, as humans, we are wired to instinctively want to be part of something, a community that allows us to demonstrate our authenticity through our unique thoughts and skills.

One way to remember the difference between the two is that "delegation is transactional while empowerment is transformational." Remember back to the Efficient Frontier of Teaming in the earlier chapter, where you were challenged to think about the type of team you are now and the one you want to be in the future. Do you want to hold a position on a team where you just complete transactional tasks daily, seemingly "punching the clock" as a dependent team? Or do you want to contribute to a culture that spends time actively thinking of new ways to innovate, collaborate, and approach situations from a different perspective to become an empowered team?

You get to choose your path, so as they say, choose wisely.

### Top Three Actions to Empower Your Team

1.  **Delegate Responsibility with Trust.** Napoleon said, *"If you want a thing done well, do it yourself."* That mindset is poison to empowerment. Trust requires letting go even when it feels uncomfortable. Remind yourself: Your team members were hired because they're capable.

2.  **Provide Resources and Support.** Stephen Covey wrote, *"Begin with the end in mind."*[22] When you delegate, describe what success looks like. Provide the context, tools, and information people need, and remember that nobody can read your mind.

3.  **Create a Culture of Communication.** In *The Office*, Jim Halpert is told to create a "rundown" but has no idea what that means. Instead of asking, he spends the episode guessing. If you haven't seen *The Office*, head to YouTube to check it out; it might resonate with your team. Don't put your team in the same position. Encourage questions. Normalize uncertainty. Make it safe to say, *"I don't know."*

## Creating Ownership

Tom and I met while I was a leadership coach at Crown Castle, a telecommunications organization, an experience I look back on with both enthusiasm and disappointment. At one point, the organization had what it called the B3 Values instilled in the very fabric of the team. It included *Be Real, Be Accountable,* and *Be an Owner.* As a coach, these values naturally warmed my heart. When I met the leaders I would be coaching, I could tell they wore these values on their sleeves, believing in their meaning and seeking ways to help their teams consistently uphold them.

However, there was an executive leader who took it upon themselves to change these values, I feel, in an attempt to instill their own stamp on the organization rather than gathering insight from the rest of the team. They changed their values to PURPLE, with each letter representing a new value.

Instead of showing up to meetings with a sense of unity bolstered by ownership, some leaders and team members began to lose their sense of direction, leading to missed deadlines, cancelled contracts, and, ultimately, several instances of finger-pointing. These issues naturally led to a decline in client support and an inability to meet expectations, as evidenced by their quarterly numbers over the years since the shift.

Ownership cannot be discounted. When team members feel they have the power to help drive results for the organization through their actions, they show up differently. They feel more engaged, motivated, and accountable to uphold their end of the bargain. When a team member feels like their contributions will have a direct impact on the company's success, there is a higher quality of work, fewer errors, and the biggest factor of all . . . a sense of pride. Once we have instilled positive accountability and empowerment in our team's culture, it leads to greater ownership of the organization's vision, mission, and results. Here are a few outcomes you can expect from increasing your team members' sense of ownership.

## 1. Connection

More engaged, invested team members lead to increased productivity. Did you know that in Gallup's latest annual employee engagement research, only 23 percent of employees globally are truly engaged?[23] This means that only a quarter of employees feel enthusiastic about their work, which matches the all-time high seen in 2022, and that personally makes me sad. Furthermore, 62 percent of employees are not engaged, and 15 percent are actively disengaged, leading to the terms "quiet quitting" and "loud quitting" respectively.

If your team members are not connected to the meaning of their roles, if they do not feel empowered, if they feel they are not there to be "owners" of what the organization is looking to accomplish, one of two outcomes can occur over time.

- Option 1: They do only what is required, avoid initiative, contribute less creativity, and stop bringing their authentic strengths to the team.
- Option 2: They actively seek other roles, become vocal about their dissatisfaction, or exit the organization entirely, taking their potential, institutional knowledge, and momentum with them.

## 2. Decision Making

Better decision-making and problem-solving are other products of increased ownership within the organization. Teams can sometimes struggle to make effective and timely decisions when they lack an emotional connection or intrinsic motivation to take initiative. When your team members are given permission to take ownership, it fosters an atmosphere of responsibility, characterized by a higher level of thoughtfulness and strategic thinking to support informed decisions.

Members of the team feel connected and confident that they are not just punching a time clock. Their work has meaning, and they know their actions add value to the team as a whole. As a bonus, the team members will be more likely to utilize their full repertoire of skills.

## 3. Innovation and Creativity

When team members are given additional responsibility, they are more likely to break out of their old ways of thinking and infuse their projects with creativity. When you encourage ownership, you provide a platform for your employees to contribute their thoughts, experiences, and ideas. It becomes more exciting for them because they can think freely and experiment with their ideas.

Ninety-seven percent of employees surveyed in the Gallup Employee Workplace study said they are more likely to stay with an organization that encourages ownership. It's the meaningless tasks and unnecessary dictatorship that drive employees out the door. Most people want to feel like they are contributing to society and at home, so why would it be any different in the workplace?

## Pulling It All Together

In today's workplace, research tells a story and, in most cases, paints a picture of a lack of positive accountability and empowerment, which has at times created a low rate of ownership among team members. As we've discussed, there is a lack of understanding of accountability and its definition in your organization. Because of this, it can be received negatively by your team.

Be honest and ask yourself whether you contribute to a negative feeling around accountability. Whether you are a leader or a team member, it is important to develop self-awareness, and the first step is to get curious about your past management style.

How are you approaching empowerment? Is it at the top of your mind and felt throughout your team's culture, or do you struggle to let go of control, seeing things through a transactional lens rather than a transformational one? I've witnessed many leaders discover learned behaviors that no longer serve them in today's workplace. It's not their fault. They simply didn't know there was another way. Inspiration comes from seeing how these leaders change their path and adopt the rules that work.

It is time for change.

Research and surveys reveal a story of discontent and disengagement among team members worldwide. We need to develop our self-awareness and learn how to show up with positivity while still holding ourselves and our team members accountable. Focusing on the attributes of positive accountability and empowerment can lead to greater ownership, which will not only drive quantitative results but also, as a byproduct, enhance engagement, innovation, creativity, and pride. Author Jim Collins discusses these factors in his book, *Good to Great.*[24]

If your culture is struggling, start by reflecting on your mindset:

- Are you using accountability as a threat or an invitation?
- Are you empowering or micromanaging?
- Are you creating clarity or confusion?

Ownership starts with self-awareness and grows through consistent action.

## Conclusion

Positive accountability and empowerment are the foundation of ownership. When people feel trusted and supported, they stop waiting to be told what to do. They step up, create solutions, and take pride in the results. It's pretty cool to witness the transformation within teams and their leaders as they instill the attributes that drive consistent ownership. Focus on the attributes discussed in this chapter by devising a game plan to elevate the team's skills. Hold a meeting together and reflect on the following questions:

- How do I currently define accountability and empowerment?
- What changes could I make to encourage ownership?
- When have I seen the power of ownership firsthand?
- What steps will I take to build this culture?

That's when work becomes more than a job. It becomes a shared mission worth showing up for every day.

## Taking Action

- Define positive accountability together as a team.
- Clarify what empowerment looks like in practice.
- Hold quarterly reviews to track progress.
- Celebrate progress and adjust where needed.

# CHAPTER 6

## It's Not About You:
## The New Model of Leadership

*I will not follow where the path may lead, but I will go where
there is no path, and I will leave a trail.*
—Muriel Strode

## What Shaped Your Leadership?

When you think about your relationship with leadership, what
has inspired and shaped your behaviors and habits? Who has
had the greatest impact on you? Maybe you learned from someone who dedicated their life to helping others reach their full
potential. Or perhaps you were shaped by a negative experience,
like the leader who repeatedly said, "We've always done it this
way," anytime someone challenged the status quo.

Today, there's a crisis of leadership in organizations. Gallup
found that only 20 percent of employees trust the leadership of
their organization.[25] Leaders account for nearly 70 percent of
the variance in their team's engagement. Yet 84 percent of companies still prioritize leadership development.[26] The paradox is
that budgets are increasing, but results aren't improving. If the
old models of leadership were working, trust and engagement

wouldn't be at historic lows. Something fundamental needs to change.

## Introduction to the Collective Leadership Model

Leadership is not a static position or a title bestowed by organizational hierarchy. At its most impactful, leadership is a dynamic, collective capacity expressed through a team's relationships, mindsets, and practices. In earlier chapters, we examined how engagement and authenticity form the efficient frontier of teaming, where performance and well-being are maximized. This chapter advances that discussion by introducing the Collective Leadership Model—a framework for cultivating five interdependent attributes that enable teams to lead together.

When teams move beyond transactional interactions and embrace collective leadership, they unlock a deeper reservoir of trust, resilience, and creativity. They begin to see their work as a shared endeavor rather than a series of delegated tasks. They lean into challenges together and grow in ways no single leader could orchestrate alone. This chapter explores what it means to deliberately build this capability, including practical strategies you can apply with your team.

## From Individual Leadership to Collective Capacity

Too often, leaders default to behaviors that feel safe. They rely on authority rather than curiosity. They confuse control with influence. They cling to the familiar rather than adapt to the needs of a changing workplace. Tom and I believe everyone's relationship to leadership is always personal. Every individual brings their personal experiences to their work, shaped by the examples set by parents, teachers, and past bosses. We either replicate those examples or consciously choose to lead differently.

Traditional leadership development focuses on individual competencies such as strategic thinking, decisiveness, and emotional intelligence. These skills matter, but they are not enough on their own. A team that depends on a single strong leader may achieve temporary success, but it is unlikely to sustain high performance over time. Collective leadership creates continuity and adaptability. When every team member practices leadership, they take initiative, offer perspective, and hold themselves accountable so that the team becomes more than the sum of its parts.

Collective leadership is not about flattening hierarchy for the sake of egalitarian ideals. It is about recognizing that leadership emerges through the quality of interactions and the shared commitment to purpose, not merely through position or authority. A culture of collective leadership holds space for candid dialogue, diverse thinking, and a bias toward action.

The model presented here emerged from observing teams across industries and contexts: healthcare organizations grappling with complexity, professional services firms navigating rapid change, and startups balancing innovation and execution. In each case, the teams that thrived consistently demonstrated five attributes in their daily practices. These attributes—Curiosity, Collaboration, Appreciation, Adaptability, and Ownership—form the backbone of the Collective Leadership Model.

| Individual Leadership | Collective Leadership |
| --- | --- |
| **Mindset Shift:** "From Me to We" | |
| • Authority-centered | • Capacity-centered |
| • Leader as decision-maker | • Leadership distributed |
| • Control and direction | • Influence and contribution |
| • Success depends on the leader | • Success sustained by the system |

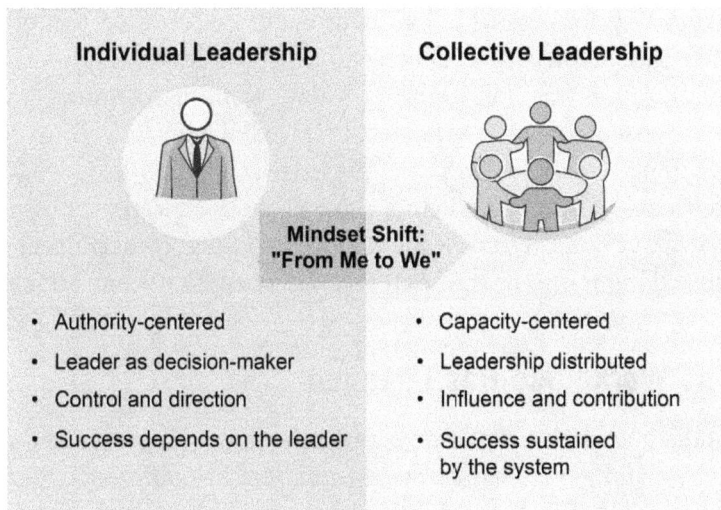

**Figure 6.1: Mindset Shift to Collective Leadership**

# Personal Experiences Shape Perspective

My father had strict rules when I was growing up. He went straight from high school into the military, and that discipline carried over into our family, shaping my early understanding of leadership with a "command and control" approach.

When I first became a leader, I copied that style. I could take charge in a crisis, work long hours, and solve problems quickly. It earned me promotions, recognition, and even additional compensation. But over time, I realized that what worked in emergencies didn't build sustainable trust. My approach sometimes shut people down rather than drawing them in, so what worked in a crisis didn't work as well in other situations.

At Wells Fargo Advisors, I witnessed firsthand how leadership can crumble under pressure. When the fraudulent account scandal broke, our CEO publicly denied wrongdoing, even though investigations revealed the behavior had been happening for years. He had built a culture based on compliance rather than trust. When the crisis hit, leaders across the organization were left in the dark along with their teams.

I coached leaders who felt betrayed. They showed up to coaching sessions asking me, "Bryan, why should I keep working here?" Those experiences showed me that leadership isn't just about skills; it's more about mindset, values, ownership, and the willingness to be transparent, even when it's uncomfortable.

## The Workplace Has Changed

Today's workplace spans five generations working together in hybrid and global teams. Each generation has different expectations. The Silent Generation grew up with "command and control," a management style where leaders make all the decisions. Millennials and Gen Z expect inclusivity, transparency, and purpose. Leadership isn't one-size-fits-all. The best teams create a shared leadership mindset.

Leaders who cling to old models of authority are out of touch with reality. Research shows that similarity creates comfort, but diversity drives growth.[27] If leaders can appreciate what each generation brings, they create a richer culture.

The world of work isn't static. Leadership can't be either.

The workplace has changed dramatically over the years. We have remote and hybrid team members around the globe and across cultures, each bringing a set of unique strengths and skills acquired through their distinct experiences and perspectives, and their authenticity only emerges when it is consistently cultivated and supported. The real obstacle is overcoming the clash between outdated leadership habits and the mindset shifts required to build a culture where empowered teammates can thrive. We are on the cusp of change.

In this area, Tom and I suggest holding conversations with all team members, either together or in one-on-one discussions. The realization that a "one size fits all" style of leadership doesn't fit today's work environment should come across from these conversations. Be curious together about what would work for the team and how you would all contribute. Hold each other accountable for demonstrating a cohesive leadership structure that applies different theories as needed.

In addition, there is no finish line for the growth and development of leadership skills. Carve out consistent time to reflect, learn, and apply new skills together as a unified group. Instead of assuming only formal leaders have authority, everyone is invited to contribute. It doesn't mean everyone leads all the time; it means everyone shares ownership.

## Lessons from Lasso

I must admit I am a latecomer to the hit show *Ted Lasso*. I was presenting to a team last year and made a comment, to which one of the members responded, "You just Ted Lassoed us." I was confused. I had not yet taken the time to watch the show; I thought it would be another SNL sketch that they stretched into a series.

My wife sat down with me when I returned from the trip, and we watched the first episode, mostly out of curiosity about what I had done to provoke the team member's comment. I was instantly drawn in as we watched episode after episode, picking our favorite characters. Mine is Roy, whom I now claim as a kindred spirit. Of the leadership lessons the show focused on, three stood out as proof that everyone should take responsibility as a leader.

### 1. Humility

Ted enters a world he doesn't understand, becoming the head coach of a European football club after coaching an American college football team, yet he doesn't pretend to know everything. He asks questions and listens. Over time, his openness transforms a skeptical team. At times, leaders in this situation might feel the need to adopt a forceful approach, thinking they must prove their knowledge to lead the team.

Ted does the exact opposite, showing humility by discussing his lack of knowledge, creating an environment where this trait begins to take hold (see Jamie Tartt from season 1 to season 3). As the locker room shifts from individuals attempting to outshine one another to an environment of collaboration, team members begin to "Believe" in each other. Here are some questions to spark your curiosity about how you can build on this in your leadership style.

### Reflection

- What do I need to do to let go of my ego and the feeling that I need to know everything for the team?
- How can I allow myself permission to ask for ideas from my team members?
- What steps can I take to create an environment where everyone feels they have permission to contribute?

## 2. Vulnerability

Traditional leaders hide their insecurities. Ted shares them. When he's transparent about what he doesn't know, it gives others permission to do the same. How many leaders have you worked for in the past who felt they had to be the rock for the team, showing no weakness, as if it was their responsibility to be strong for everyone else? This adage has seen its last days, as team members today seek leaders who can show that failures are inevitable.

## Reflection

- What challenges could I share with the team?
- How can I create a safe environment for others to be vulnerable?
- What can I do to ask for feedback and set the tone for the team in this area?

## 3. Courage

Great teams resist groupthink. They create space for dissent and debate. One of my coaching mantras is: *Say what you need to say, not what others want to hear.* When coaching leaders and their teams, this is one of the most difficult things to consistently put into practice.

This is one of the areas that teams struggle to implement consistently, but when done well, it can lead to increased accountability, ownership, and empowerment among all team members.

Find the courage to show up, be open, and be objective so that the team can value the creativity and diversity of thought and experience around them. Here are a few questions to spark your curiosity as you consider incorporating courage into your leadership style.

## Reflection

- How can I encourage my team to speak up, even when it's uncomfortable?
- What steps can I take to model courage?
- What do we need to engage in healthy debate or productive conflict?

The ability to shift from the perception that a leader must show strength and is not allowed to have faults to one that celebrates open discussions is truly inspiring. There's something special about working with leaders who have found the ability to be their authentic selves in the workplace, setting a tone for their team members where it's permissible to demonstrate humility, vulnerability, and courage.

In addition, leadership is a skill anyone on the team can develop because it's not just one person's responsibility. Tom and I want you to think about how, regardless of your role, you can show up differently by sharing this responsibility across the team, especially when you are focused on raising the authenticity of each individual and the different thoughts, traits, and skills they bring to the collective.

I challenge that Coach Lasso might have found the "BBQ sauce" for leaders to change their mindset to celebrate support rather than condemn weakness. And in the words of Roy, my self-proclaimed kindred spirit: WHISTLE!

## Leadership Theories to Guide You

It is time to be curious about how to build a culture of leadership with the expectation that everyone can contribute so that there are no gaps or bottlenecks, which is one of the areas that moves a dependent team to an empowered one. A leadership culture is one that shapes behaviors in which everyone feels responsible for leading when called upon. Thus, it creates a mindset of leadership rather than just a set of skills or learned behaviors.

In this next section, we will explore some of the popular leadership theories. We want you to create a culture where you establish a leadership mindset and a standard of care grounded in values, needs, and alignment with everyone involved.

As Tom and I mentioned, each generation of team members wants to be heard and respected, especially when building a strong leadership presence on a team where everyone leads when called upon. Here are just a few leadership theories to discuss with your team members.

## 1. Authentic Leadership

Built on integrity, transparency, and empathy. During the pandemic, authentic leaders admitted uncertainty and built trust in the process. Authentic leaders showed they were unsure of what was to come, leading their teams through one of the toughest times in recent history. They were open and sincere in their communication with team members, which built long-lasting relationships through the trust they earned. Traits such as integrity, transparency, and empathy, along with your ability to communicate with your team confidently through those traits, form the foundation of authentic leadership. Now the call to action is clear: practice these behaviors consistently, invite honest dialogue, and model the courage you expect from your team. This is how trust becomes a daily habit rather than a reaction to crisis.

### Reflection

- What would happen if I were more transparent with my team?
- How could my team respond if I modeled empathy and vulnerability?
- What would be the result of being more transparent?

## 2. Transformational Leadership

Tom and I have a bias toward this one. Every time we meet a leader who has evolved to a point where they feel comfortable empowering their team members, I'm in awe. Transformational leaders can instill a culture of engagement and inspiration because they tend to focus on how they can motivate members of their team to reach their full potential.[28]

They are big on creating vision statements with meaning, so there is a sort of North Star the team can aspire to achieve in the future. Team members are energized and engaged to support the organization's results and feel connected to the mission when they have a transformational leader. Remember the Efficient Frontier of Teaming model and how the team can move from a dependent to an empowered team. This could serve as an important piece along that journey.

### Reflection

- What vision could inspire my team?
- How can we create an environment of empowerment?
- What steps can we take as a team to feel more connected to our purpose?

## 3. Inclusive Leadership Theory

This leadership theory is first attributed to authors Ingrid Nembhard and Amy Edmondson.[29] It focuses on including and valuing each team member's diverse perspectives and backgrounds. I often ask my teams how they consistently incorporate the diversity of knowledge and experience.

This theory is built on the foundation of creating an inclusive team culture where everyone is celebrated for their uniqueness and contributions to the team dynamic. These leaders are self-aware and consistently invest time in understanding their team's culture, knowledge, and experiences to cultivate inclusive environments. Research shows that having a truly diverse and inclusive team leads to higher performance.[30]

Does this leadership style fit you? Ask yourself the following questions.

## Reflection

- How do we create a culture that values every team member's voice?
- What can we do to celebrate and appreciate our different experiences and points of view?
- What would be the result of having an inclusive environment on the team?

## 4. Servant Leadership

There is so much to appreciate about Robert Greenleaf's leadership theory. Since it was developed at a time when command-and-control was the prevailing approach for most organizations, his concepts radically shifted the dynamics of what leadership meant and what those who led aspired to be. When this theory was introduced, it focused on ten competencies, or tenets, as he called them.

### Robert Greenleaf's Ten Tenets of Servant Leadership

| Tenet | Description |
| --- | --- |
| Listening | Commitment to hearing and understanding others. |
| Empathy | Understanding and sharing others' feelings. |
| Healing | Helping people overcome challenges. |
| Awareness | Being attuned to self and surroundings. |
| Persuasion | Influencing through dialogue, not force. |
| Conceptualization | Envisioning long-term possibilities. |
| Foresight | Predicting outcomes using past and present. |
| Stewardship | Caring for the organization as a whole. |
| Growth | Supporting others' development. |
| Building Community | Creating belonging and connection. |

### Figure 6.2: Ten Tenets of Servant Leadership

When you pull these areas together, the leader's focus shifts to the needs and well-being of their team members over their own personal gain. They show up fully present for those they lead, demonstrating competencies such as listening, a skill that is rare among leaders, unfortunately. There is a lot to appreciate about servant leadership; a lot of work and effort go into learning and practicing its tenets, as these are not check-the-box skills.

Although most are qualitative in nature, they can sometimes be the missing pieces that help a team perform at an optimal level. When discussing leadership from a servant's point of view, here are a few points to discuss with your team members.

### Reflection

- Which of these tenets would be the strengths of the team?

- Which one or two would be opportunities for us to improve?
- How could we adopt a collective focus on becoming a servant leadership team?

## The Power of Collective Leadership

This is a concept that Tom and I discuss when coaching and consulting teams. Throughout this chapter, we discussed a shift in mindset for leadership. No longer is it to be displayed by one individual or those with a manager title. The power is in everyone having accountability to lead when needed. Moving toward an empowered team means removing roadblocks that can arise, such as moments when team members wait before acting or when teams feel they have no choice but to rely on others for direction.

Empowered teams can hold discussions together and design their future as a collective, which is why the title is Collective Leadership. They provide an environment where everyone on the team feels they can contribute to the leadership mantra. I am reminded of the Three Musketeers and their motto, "One for all and all for one." Collective leadership is about curiosity, collaboration, appreciation, adaptability, and having an ownership mindset that you can create as a team.

Instead of leading from the past, this is an opportunity for everyone to share the responsibility of creating the future. Imagine a world where everyone supports a leadership mindset, where employees work together to build a strong team rather than have one person dictate how things should go based on their past experiences.

As a team, we can create our own picture of what leadership means to everyone involved, how we will commit to adapting to those needs, and the ownership to learn new behaviors together so that we can truly create something to be proud of. If all goes according to plan, this mindset will become embedded in the organization's DNA and culture. Let's review the traits of Collective Leadership to support this mindset, so the team can paint the sky in new and exciting ways, tailored to each other's needs.

## The Collective Leadership Model

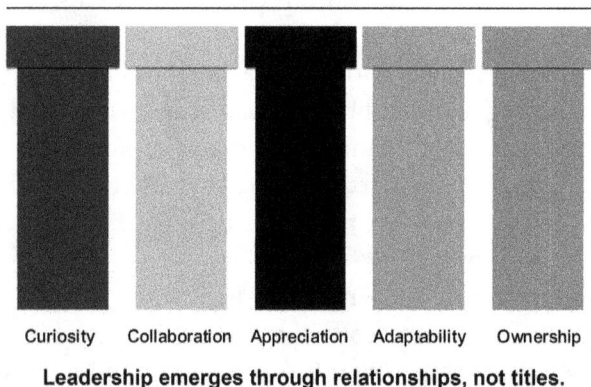

**Collective Leadership**

Curiosity   Collaboration   Appreciation   Adaptability   Ownership

**Leadership emerges through relationships, not titles.**

Figure 6.3: The Collective Leadership Model

## The Collective Leadership Concept

Most leadership books focus on the individual. From our experience, Tom and I have seen that the most resilient teams co-create their leadership culture. Focus on identifying the leadership styles each team member brings to the collective. How can you appreciate their strengths, and when can they step up and lead? Who on the team can provide structure during a crisis? Which team member values inclusivity and can support the rest of the team in keeping this in mind?

This framework is more about awareness of the team's leadership strengths and applying them as a group when needed. Review the following traits together as a team.

**Collective Leadership is focused on the following traits:**

- **Curiosity:** Letting go of certainty and exploring together.
- **Collaboration:** Valuing every perspective.
- **Appreciation:** Celebrating what makes us different.
- **Adaptability:** Shifting styles based on the moment.
- **Ownership:** Taking responsibility collectively.

## Table 6.1: The Collective Leadership Model

| Attribute | Description |
|---|---|
| Curiosity | The mindset of exploring ideas without judgment, inviting questions, and seeking to understand rather than assume. |
| Collaboration | The practice of co-creating solutions by combining perspectives, skills, and efforts toward a shared purpose. |
| Appreciation | The discipline of recognizing value in each person's contribution and expressing gratitude consistently. |
| Adaptability | The capacity to adjust approaches, roles, and expectations fluidly in response to changing circumstances. |
| Ownership | The commitment to personal accountability and collective responsibility for the team's outcomes. |

## Curiosity: Exploring Without Assumption

Curiosity is the mindset of exploration. It is the discipline of asking questions, not to confirm biases but to uncover new possibilities. Curious teams resist the temptation to assume they already understand every angle. They remain open to each member's unique insights and challenge each other to look beyond conventional explanations.

### Case Example

When a regional banking team faced declining client engagement, their initial instinct was to blame market trends. However, one team member, Jasmine, suggested they conduct interviews with long-term clients to understand what had changed. Through these conversations, they discovered that their service model had grown increasingly transactional, losing the personal touch that once distinguished them. This insight emerged only because Jasmine's curiosity overcame the comfort of assumptions.

### Coaching Reflection

How often do you pause to ask, "What might we be missing?" When was the last time your team challenged an established process simply to understand it better?
What signals tell you that your team's curiosity is being stifled?

### Practical Takeaway

Establish a practice of "question rounds" in meetings, where every team member contributes at least one genuine inquiry before decisions are made.

## Collaboration: Co-Creating Solutions

Collaboration is more than cooperation. It is the practice of co-creating, where individuals contribute distinct expertise and perspectives to shape outcomes together. In collective leadership, collaboration becomes the norm rather than the exception.

### Case Example

An engineering firm preparing for a major product launch encountered a critical design flaw weeks before release. Instead of escalating blame or retreating into silos, the team convened a cross-functional working session. Designers, engineers, and product managers worked together to map out scenarios, identify constraints, and develop a revised solution within 72 hours. Their capacity to collaborate quickly and effectively was the product of deliberate investment in trust and transparency.

### Coaching Reflection

What conditions make it easy or hard for your team to collaborate?
Are contributions weighted by rank or by relevance?
Where could you create more space for co-creation?

### Practical Takeaway

Use visual planning tools like kanban boards or shared whiteboards to make progress visible and contributions transparent.

## Appreciation: Recognizing and Valuing Contributions

Appreciation is the discipline of seeing and acknowledging the value each person brings. It goes beyond occasional praise to create a culture where contributions are noticed, named, and celebrated. Appreciation fuels engagement and reinforces trust.

### Case Example

In a large healthcare system, a nursing team implemented a "daily gratitude huddle." Each morning, team members shared one example of a colleague's contribution that made a difference. Over time, this practice not only improved morale but also strengthened collaboration and reduced turnover.

### Coaching Reflection

How consistently do you and your team acknowledge each other's efforts?
What practices help you recognize less visible contributions?
How could you make appreciation part of your team's rhythm?

### Practical Takeaway

Introduce a structured practice—such as weekly recognition highlights—to normalize appreciation as part of the workflow.

## Adaptability: Navigating Change Fluidly

Adaptability is the capacity to shift roles, expectations, and approaches in response to new information and evolving circumstances. Collectively adaptive teams don't panic in the face of ambiguity—they reorient together.

### Case Example

During the early months of the COVID-19 pandemic, a nonprofit organization had to pivot from in-person events to virtual programming almost overnight. The team set up short, frequent check-ins to assess what was working and what wasn't. They embraced imperfect experiments and iterated rapidly. This adaptability not only kept the organization afloat but also expanded its reach to new audiences.

### Coaching Reflection

How does your team talk about change? Are they narratives of loss or of learning?
How do you respond when plans unravel?
What signals tell you it's time to adapt?

### Practical Takeaway

Create decision-making thresholds: criteria that clarify when you pivot, persevere, or pause.

## Ownership: Committing to Shared Accountability

Ownership is the commitment to personal accountability and collective responsibility. In collective leadership, ownership means each team member feels responsible not only for their tasks but also for the team's shared outcomes.

### Case Example

A consulting team developed a practice of "collective retrospectives" after every major engagement. Instead of focusing solely on individual performance, they reviewed what the team did well, what they missed, and the commitments they would make moving forward. Over time, this practice fostered a shared sense of accountability, thereby improving project outcomes.

### Coaching Reflection

What does ownership look like in your team's daily behaviors?
How do you model accountability as a leader?
Where are you unintentionally signaling that responsibility belongs elsewhere?

### Practical Takeaway

Embed shared accountability practices, such as collective reviews or peer feedback, into your team's routines.

# Bringing It All Together

The Collective Leadership Model is not a checklist to be completed; it is a living system of practices and mindsets. When teams invest in curiosity, they unlock insight. When they collaborate deeply, they build solutions that no one person could design alone. When they appreciate each other, they reinforce trust. When they adapt, they remain resilient. When they own their shared work, they move with purpose.

Consider where your team already demonstrates these attributes and where there are opportunities to grow. Begin by introducing small practices, such as question rounds, gratitude huddles, and decision thresholds, to reinforce the mindsets you want to cultivate. Over time, these practices become habits, and habits become culture.

Collective leadership is the engine of sustainable performance. It is how teams endure uncertainty and complexity while preserving their humanity and connection. As you continue this journey, remember that your role is not to have all the answers but to create the conditions for leadership to emerge everywhere. Leadership isn't a title. It's a mindset. When you embrace humility, vulnerability, and courage, it creates space for others to do the same, unlocking the potential of everyone around you.

Remember: It's not about you. It's about what you can build together.

## Taking Action

- Map each team member's leadership strengths.
- Reflect on your personal stories of good and bad leadership.
- Create a team contract outlining how you'll practice Collective Leadership.
- Revisit it quarterly.

# CHAPTER 7

## The Safe Space: Creating an Environment of Trust and Psychological Safety

*Psychological safety is a shared belief that the team is safe for interpersonal risk-taking. It is a sense of confidence that the team will not embarrass, reject, or punish someone for speaking up.*
—Amy C. Edmondson

### Introduction: From Collective Leadership to Collective Courage

In Chapter 6, we explored the Collective Leadership Model and the five core attributes that enable teams to transcend transactional work and achieve something more resilient, adaptive, and fulfilling. We saw how Curiosity, Collaboration, Appreciation, Adaptability, and Ownership together form a system of leadership that can outlast any one person's authority.

Now we dive into the deeper foundation beneath all those attributes, where something so essential is present that, without it, even the best-intentioned efforts fall flat. That foundation is psychological safety.

You can have a team with clear goals, a shared purpose, and sophisticated collaboration tools. You can have highly skilled leaders who are technically excellent and intellectually capable, but if people don't feel safe to show up fully, to disagree, to question, and to reveal their uncertainties, you will never realize the potential of collective leadership. You'll have a room full of smart people nodding along, careful not to step on toes, while big problems go unspoken.

This chapter is about creating that foundation: the conditions that make it safe to speak up, to test assumptions, and to challenge one another without devolving into blame or hostility. Psychological safety is often misunderstood. Some leaders hear the term and think it means coddling or lowering the bar for accountability. But the opposite is true. When people feel safe, they are more willing to stretch themselves, take risks, and hold each other to higher standards because they trust that their value is not contingent on being perfect.

In many ways, psychological safety is the invisible force that binds together the other attributes of collective leadership. It is what allows curiosity to flourish instead of fizzling into polite avoidance. It's what turns collaboration from superficial cooperation into genuine co-creation. It appreciates the weight of sincerity, makes adaptability less threatening, and transforms ownership from a defensive posture into a shared commitment. This chapter will show you what psychological safety really looks like in practice, how to build it deliberately, and what it takes to sustain it when the pressure is on.

## Cultivating the Right Kind of Friction

If you observe high-performing teams over time, you will notice something paradoxical: they are not always comfortable with each other. In fact, many of them regularly engage in robust, sometimes heated debates about ideas, priorities, and strategies.

They challenge one another's assumptions, question proposals, and point out flaws. But underneath all that friction is a steady current of respect and trust.

That is the heart of psychological safety: the ability to separate the friction of ideas from the friction of relationships.[31]

Too often, leaders think the opposite. They assume that if people disagree, the team must be unsafe. Or if the tone is smooth and harmonious, the team must be healthy. But surface harmony can be misleading. Sometimes it's just conflict avoidance.

Let's define two kinds of friction that frequently get tangled together.

**Social friction** happens when disagreements feel personal. It shows up as resentment, judgment, or withdrawal. When social friction is high, people start to question whether they belong or whether their perspectives are respected.

**Intellectual friction** happens when people are encouraged to vigorously challenge ideas. It shows up as debate, curiosity, and respectful dissent. When intellectual friction is high and social friction is low, teams innovate faster because everyone feels safe to contribute.

## Table 7.1: The Two Types of Friction

|  | LOW INTELLECTUAL FRICTION | HIGH INTELLECTUAL FRICTION |
|---|---|---|
| LOW SOCIAL FRICTION | Indifferent & Disengaged | **Psychological Safety (Ideal Zone)** |
| HIGH SOCIAL FRICTION | Friendly but Stagnant | Conflictual & Unproductive |

Most teams hover in the bottom left quadrant—friendly but stagnant. People like each other well enough, but they don't challenge each other's ideas with much rigor. They confuse politeness for trust, when trust requires enough safety to risk disagreement.

## Case Example: The Global Product Team

A few years ago, I worked with a global technology company's product team that had a reputation for collegiality. Everyone was courteous, meetings were orderly, and conflict was rare. On the surface, it looked like a model culture. Then a new VP joined. She was strategic, ambitious, and unafraid to challenge conventional thinking. At first, people nodded along in meetings. But as her ideas pushed the team into uncomfortable territory, something changed.

Engineers stopped voicing their concerns. Product managers deferred decisions they would normally own. Deadlines slipped, but no one spoke up.

Eventually, in an off-site, one senior engineer admitted he had stopped sharing feedback. "I didn't want to be the guy who always disagreed," he said. "It started to feel like questioning anything would be taken as resistance."

That admission cracked open the conversation. The VP realized her forceful advocacy was creating social friction she didn't intend. The team had been conflating disagreement with disloyalty, and it took a deliberate conversation to untangle them.

## The Upward Spiral of Trust

When people talk about trust, they often imagine it as a static quality: something you either have or don't, though in reality, it is dynamic. It evolves through repeated cycles of vulnerability and response. Each time someone takes a small risk, shares an unpopular idea, admits a mistake, and is met with respect rather than blame, trust grows a little deeper.

Over time, these moments compound into what I call the **upward spiral of trust**.[32]

It starts small. A team member asks a question they're worried might sound naive. Another offers a dissenting perspective. Someone else flags a potential risk that everyone else overlooked. Each of these actions tests the environment. When leaders respond with curiosity rather than criticism, the team learns that speaking up is safe. Trust doesn't mean you always agree. In fact, the strongest teams often have the most robust debates. They trust that their relationships can withstand honest disagreement. They trust that no single comment will define them in their colleagues' eyes.

Consider a marketing director I coached named Lila. When she joined a new organization, she noticed that her team rarely challenged one another. In weekly meetings, everyone shared updates, but no one asked probing questions. Lila decided to model what healthy dissent could look like.

In one meeting, after a presentation on a major campaign, she thanked the team member for their work and then said, "I have some questions because I want to make sure we're not missing anything. Would it be alright if I push on a few assumptions?" She then offered three thoughtful critiques—without apologizing or diluting her perspective.

The presenter nodded, engaged with her questions, and the rest of the team began to chime in. Over time, this simple practice normalized curiosity and debate. Months later, a colleague told her, "You helped us realize disagreement doesn't mean disrespect."

This is the upward spiral of trust in action: each small risk taken and met with respect builds a stronger foundation for the next conversation.

## Four Core Skills for Building Psychological Safety

Psychological safety isn't created by wishful thinking or generic encouragement. It requires specific behaviors that can be practiced over time. While many skills contribute to an environment of safety, I've found that **four core capabilities** have an outsized impact:

- Shifting from Judgment to Curiosity
- Identifying Emotions
- Landing the Plane
- Reality Testing

In this section, we'll explore the first two. In the next step, we'll dive into the last two and discuss how to put all of them into practice.

### Four Core Skills for Psychological Safety

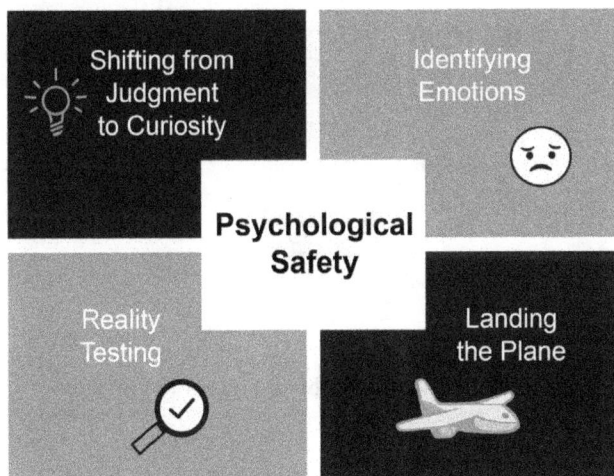

Figure 7.2: Four Core Skills for Psychological Safety

## Skill #1: Shifting from Judgment to Curiosity

When a team member does something you don't understand, misses a deadline, resists a change, or fails to contribute, it's easy to leap to judgment. You assume they're lazy, uncommitted, or incompetent. But judgment closes the door to learning. Curiosity holds it open. Shifting from judgment to curiosity is a practice of mental reframing. It means noticing your assumptions and replacing them with questions.

### Example

**Judgment:** "Michael never prepares for meetings. He doesn't care."

**Curiosity:** "What gets in the way of Michael preparing? Have we been clear about expectations? Does he have the context he needs?"

## Shift from Judgment to Curiosity

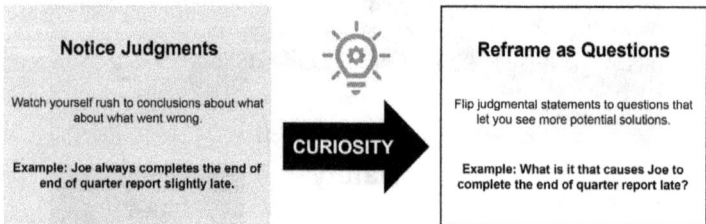

| Notice Judgments | | Reframe as Questions |
|---|---|---|
| Watch yourself rush to conclusions about what about what went wrong. | CURIOSITY | Flip judgmental statements to questions that let you see more potential solutions. |
| Example: Joe always completes the end of end of quarter report slightly late. | | Example: What is it that causes Joe to complete the end of quarter report late? |

Figure 7.3: Transition from Judgment to Curiosity

This shift doesn't mean you excuse poor performance. It simply means you start by seeking to understand before you reach a conclusion. In a software development team I worked with, the manager, Tanya, was frustrated that a senior engineer always seemed disengaged in sprint planning. She assumed he was checked out. But when she paused to ask herself, "What else could be true?" she realized she had never asked him directly what he needed to participate fully.

In their next one-on-one, she shared her observation and asked an open question. It turned out he felt uncomfortable contributing because he lacked clarity on customer requirements and didn't want to derail discussions by asking "basic" questions. Together, they created a plan to provide better pre-meeting context.

### Coaching Prompt

The next time you feel judgment bubbling up, pause. Write down the thought. Then reframe it as a question. Notice how your mindset shifts when you approach the situation as a learner rather than a critic.

## Skill #2: Identifying Emotions

Emotions are the undercurrent of every conversation. When you can name them both in yourself and in others, you bring clarity to what's happening beneath the surface. This skill transforms vague discomfort into actionable understanding. Most teams use a limited vocabulary for feelings: "frustrated," "stressed," "happy," or "disappointed." But there is enormous power in identifying more nuanced emotions. Naming an experience accurately defuses its intensity.

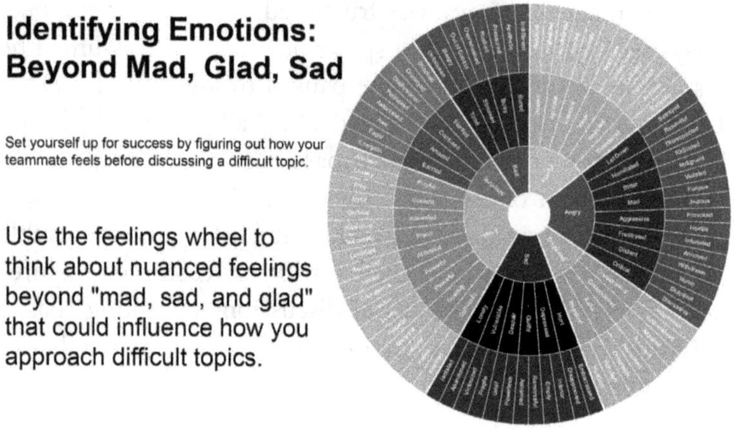

## Identifying Emotions: Beyond Mad, Glad, Sad

Set yourself up for success by figuring out how your teammate feels before discussing a difficult topic.

Use the feelings wheel to think about nuanced feelings beyond "mad, sad, and glad" that could influence how you approach difficult topics.

**Figure 7.4: Emotions Wheel**

### Example

During a project debrief, a team member might say, "I'm frustrated about how this went." You can help them get more specific by gently prompting, "What kind of frustration? Is it disappointment, resentment, or feeling overlooked?"

By teasing apart those distinctions, you uncover valuable information:

- **Disappointment** often signals unmet expectations.
- **Resentment** may point to a feeling of injustice or imbalance.
- **Feeling overlooked** can indicate a lack of recognition.

In one executive team, a VP was habitually terse in meetings. Her colleagues interpreted this as disengagement, but when the CEO finally asked, "What are you feeling when we talk about these topics?" she admitted, "I'm afraid I'm not adding value." That admission shifted the entire team's perception. Instead of judging her as aloof, they understood her behavior as being rooted in anxiety.

### Coaching Prompt

Keep a list of feeling words in your notebook or on your phone. In your next meeting, try to identify at least three specific emotions you notice in the room.

Practice reflecting them back gently: "I'm sensing some hesitation here—does that feel accurate?"

### The Takeaway

If you want real psychological safety, you must build a culture where ideas are fair game, but people are respected. This doesn't happen by accident. It requires clear norms, skillful facilitation, and the courage to model it yourself.

## Skill #3: Landing the Plane

Many leaders have been trained to be either overly diplomatic or uncomfortably blunt. They swing between sugarcoating feedback so thoroughly that it loses impact and delivering it so forcefully that it leaves a bruise. Landing the plane means bringing difficult topics to ground clearly and respectfully. It's the discipline of balancing candor with care.

When you land the plane skillfully, you:

- Reduce ambiguity about what needs to change
- Preserve the dignity of the person receiving the feedback
- Create space for collaborative problem-solving

## Land the Plane

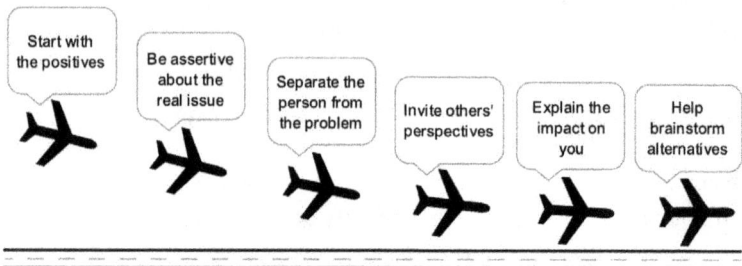

Like a pilot running through their pre-landing safety checklist, think through how to apply these 6 behaviors to land your difficult messages.

**Figure 7.5: Landing the Plane**

### The Seven Steps of Landing the Plane

Here is a structured approach you can use to prepare:

1. **Start with Positives:** Ground the conversation in appreciation for what is working.
2. **Separate the Person from the Issue:** Make it clear that the concern is about behavior or outcomes, not character.
3. **Describe What Happened:** Use objective, specific language. Avoid generalizations like "always" or "never."
4. **Explain the Impact:** Articulate why this matters to you, the team, or the client.
5. **Invite Perspectives:** Give the other person space to share their view.
6. **Be Assertive About the Real Issue:** Don't let the conversation drift into tangents. Name the core problem.
7. **Help Brainstorm Solutions:** Shift toward action and shared ownership.

## Example

Imagine you are leading a project, and a colleague repeatedly misses agreed-upon deadlines. Here's how you might land the plane:

> "I want to start by saying how much I value your creativity on this project. Your ideas have improved the deliverables, and clients have noticed. I do want to talk about something that's been challenging. In the past six weeks, three key milestones were missed. That has put the rest of the team under pressure to catch up.
>
> "When deadlines slip, it affects our credibility with the client. I'd like to hear your perspective on what's been happening. Then, let's figure out how we can get back on track."

Notice how this approach avoids blame while still naming the issue clearly.

## Common Pitfalls

Landing the plane isn't easy. Here are some patterns that derail the conversation:

> **The Soft Start That Never Lands:** You praise so thoroughly that you never get to the concern.
> **The Critical Dump:** You list every frustration you've ever had instead of focusing on the core issue.
> **The Disguised Demand:** You phrase your concern as a question but expect only one answer.

## Coaching Prompts

Before delivering feedback, rehearse your key message in one sentence. If you can't state it clearly, you're not ready.

After the conversation, reflect: Did the person understand the issue? Do they know what needs to happen next?

## Skill #4: Reality Testing

Reality testing is the practice of questioning catastrophic predictions and replacing them with data. Anxiety thrives in uncertainty. When you imagine worst-case scenarios unchecked, you are more likely to avoid critical conversations.

This skill has two parts:

> **Internal Testing:** Noticing the story you're telling yourself.
> **External Testing:** Running small experiments to see what is true.

### Example

I once coached a senior leader who was hesitant to give a team member constructive feedback. She believed, "If I bring this up, he'll get defensive and shut down. Then our relationship will be ruined." We worked through a reality-testing exercise:

**Evidence for This Prediction:** "Last year, he reacted badly to feedback."

- **Evidence Against:** "When I shared positive recognition, he was receptive. When others gave him feedback recently, he handled it well."

- **Small Experiment:** "I'll start with one specific example rather than a list and see how he responds."

When she finally raised the concern, he thanked her and asked for help improving. The catastrophic prediction never materialized.

### Practical Framework: The Reality Testing Ladder

Here is a simple tool you can use:

1. **Observation:** What did I see or hear?
2. **Interpretation:** What story am I telling about it?
3. **Prediction:** What do I think will happen if I act?
4. **Evidence:** What facts support or contradict that prediction?
5. **Experiment:** What is the smallest step I can take to test it?

This ladder helps you separate assumptions from reality, reducing fear and building confidence.

### Case Story: The Overdue Report

A project manager I worked with, Jordan, avoided addressing repeated late reports because he convinced himself the analyst would quit if confronted. His inner narrative was, "He's overworked, he's sensitive, and he'll see this as personal criticism." When we walked through the Reality Testing Ladder, Jordan realized:

- He had never actually shared that the delays were a problem.

- The analyst had stayed engaged during other difficult conversations.
- The fear was more about Jordan's discomfort than any evidence.

Jordan decided to try a low-stakes experiment: simply stating that deadlines mattered and asking for the support needed to meet them. To his surprise, the analyst appreciated the clarity and suggested a process improvement that helped everyone.

### Coaching Prompt

The next time you feel paralyzed by what-ifs, ask: "What would it look like to take one step to test this belief?" Notice what happens when you replace predictions with real-world data.

### Integrating the Four Skills

These four skills, Shifting from Judgment to Curiosity, Identifying Emotions, Landing the Plane, and Reality Testing, all work together to build psychological safety over time. Each skill reinforces the others:

- Curiosity keeps your mindset open.
- Emotional awareness creates empathy.
- Clear feedback maintains transparency.
- Reality testing calms fear.

No single skill is sufficient alone. But together, they form the backbone of cultures where people feel safe to speak up, take risks, and grow.

## A Structured Practice for Your Team

Creating psychological safety doesn't happen by intention alone, as it requires consistent practice. One of the most effective ways I've seen teams build these habits is by using a **Four-Meeting Practice Cycle**. This approach provides clear focus, manageable steps, and collective accountability. Each meeting focuses on one core skill, giving people space to experiment without pressure to master everything at once.

## The Four Meeting Practice Cycle

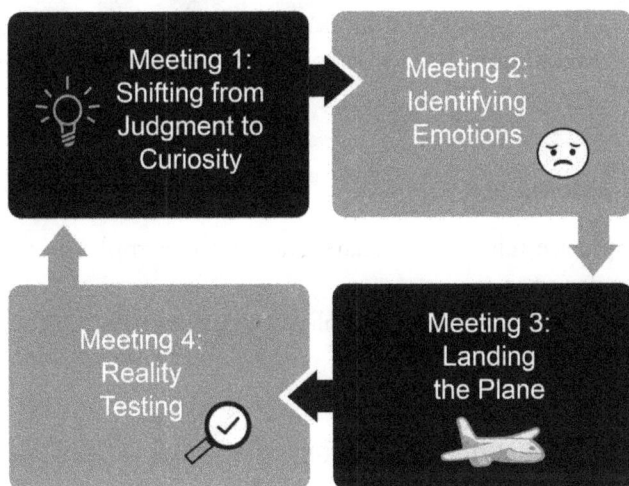

Figure 7.6: Four-Meeting Practice Cycle

- Meeting 1: Shifting from Judgment to Curiosity
- Meeting 2: Identifying Emotions
- Meeting 3: Landing the Plane
- Meeting 4: Reality Testing

## Meeting 1: Shifting from Judgment to Curiosity

**Goal:** Help the team recognize default judgments and reframe them as questions.

### How to Facilitate

- Open with a story or example of how judgment shuts down learning.
- Ask each person to share a moment when they jumped to conclusions.
- Practice reframing: "What question could you ask instead?"
- Wrap up by setting a commitment: Over the next week, notice three moments when you feel judgment and write them down.

### Troubleshooting Tips

If people are reluctant to share, start with examples from your own experience.

Avoid turning this into a blame exercise and keep the tone reflective.

## Meeting 2: Identifying Emotions

**Goal:** Develop shared language for feelings so the team can surface and name them skillfully.

### How to Facilitate

- Bring a list of nuanced emotions, like anticipation, guilt, enthusiasm, shame, and relief.

- Ask everyone to pick two emotions they've felt recently at work.
- Discuss what triggered those feelings and how they impacted behavior.
- Encourage reflection: "What would help you name these more easily in the moment?"

### Example Prompt

"When you feel anxious in a meeting, what's happening internally?" "How do you recognize that emotion before it takes over?"

## Meeting 3: Landing the Plane

**Goal:** Practice delivering clear, compassionate feedback.

### How to Facilitate

- Review the seven steps of Landing the Plane.
- Ask each person to think of a recent situation where they struggled to give feedback.
- In pairs, role-play the conversation.
- Debrief as a group: What felt natural? What felt awkward?

### Tips for Success

Reinforce that clarity is kindness—vague feedback doesn't help anyone grow.

Model the skill yourself by giving real-time coaching during the exercise.

## Meeting 4: Reality Testing

**Goal:** Challenge untested assumptions and catastrophic predictions.

### How to Facilitate

- Introduce the Reality Testing Ladder:
  - Observation
  - Interpretation
  - Prediction
  - Evidence
  - Experiment
- Invite participants to share an untested belief: "If I speak up, I'll be ignored."
- Guide them through each step of the ladder.
- Ask: "What's the smallest action you could take to test this belief?"

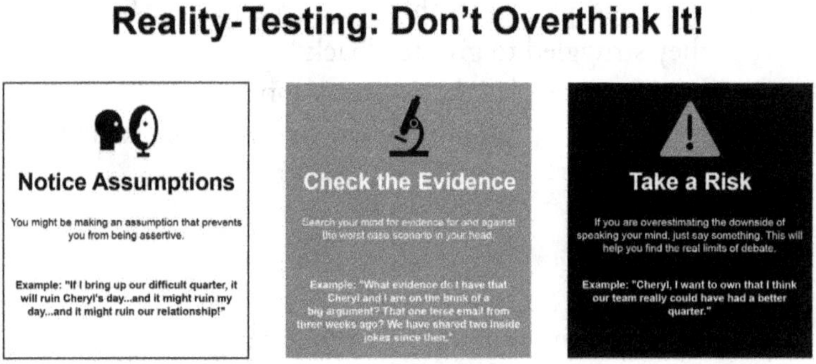

## Reality-Testing: Don't Overthink It!

**Notice Assumptions**

You might be making an assumption that prevents you from being assertive.

Example: "If I bring up our difficult quarter, it will ruin Cheryl's day...and it might ruin my day...and it might ruin our relationship!"

**Check the Evidence**

Search your mind for evidence for and against the worst case scenario in your head.

Example: "What evidence do I have that Cheryl and I are on the brink of a big argument? That one tense email from three weeks ago? We have shared two inside jokes since them."

**Take a Risk**

If you are overestimating the downside of speaking your mind, just say something. This will help you find the real limits of debate.

Example: "Cheryl, I want to own that I think our team really could have had a better quarter."

**Figure 7.7: Reality Testing**

### Practice Commitment

Over the next week, each person tries one low-risk experiment and shares the outcome.

### Implementation Guidance

- **Frequency:** Hold the meetings weekly or bi-weekly—consistency matters more than speed.
- **Facilitator Role:** You don't have to be an expert. Your job is to hold space, encourage candor, and keep the focus on learning.
- **Tracking Progress:** Consider a shared document where team members can record insights, commitments, and reflections.
- **Troubleshooting:** If participation wanes, check whether the psychological safety to experiment is in place.
- **Reiterate the purpose:** This is about building collective skill, not evaluating individual performance.

## Sustaining Psychological Safety Over Time

Embedding psychological safety isn't a one-time initiative. It's a practice that must be nurtured as the team evolves.

Here are four strategies to help you sustain it:

1. **Normalize Learning**
   Make it clear that mistakes are expected and seen as data. When something goes wrong, start with, "What can we learn?" rather than, "Who is at fault?"

2. **Ritualize Feedback**
   Build regular feedback loops into your workflow. For example:
   a. Monthly retrospectives focused on process, not people.
   b. Brief check-ins after major milestones.
3. **Model Vulnerability**
   As a leader, share your uncertainties and admit when you don't have answers. This signals that imperfection is acceptable.
4. **Celebrate Risk-Taking**
   Recognize not just successes but also thoughtful experiments—even when they fail. Reward the courage to try.

## Case Story: The Annual Review Reset

In a consulting firm I advised, the leadership team realized their annual performance reviews were undermining psychological safety. Because feedback was only formalized once a year, small issues became big problems. The process felt punitive instead of developmental.

They decided to implement quarterly check-ins with three simple questions:

- What's one thing you've done recently that you're proud of?
- What's one area where you need support to improve?
- What's one way I can help you?

Within six months, trust improved, and engagement scores rose. Regular conversations made feedback feel less loaded and more normal.

## Conclusion: The Ongoing Work of Trust

Psychological safety is not something you declare. It's something you demonstrate in every meeting, every feedback conversation, and every decision: listening before reacting. It is created in the moments when someone risks showing vulnerability and is met with respect.

Tim's team didn't transform because of a single assessment or workshop. They changed because they kept practicing. They built the courage to disagree without disconnecting. They chose curiosity over judgment, clarity over avoidance, and compassion over fear. The practices you've learned in this chapter are not quick fixes. They are invitations to keep showing up differently and to create the conditions where everyone can bring their best ideas and their most authentic selves.

In the next chapter, we'll explore how to translate this foundation of trust into systems of accountability and sustained performance, ensuring that the culture you've built not only survives but also continues to evolve as your team grows.

## Taking Action

- Where do people hesitate to speak up, and what behaviors or signals might be creating that hesitation?
- When was the last time we visibly rewarded truth-telling, vulnerability, or constructive dissent? How consistently do we model curiosity, humility, accountability, and listening without defensiveness?
- What specific commitments can we make in the next 30 days to strengthen psychological safety on our team?
- If a new team member joined tomorrow, what psychological climate would they walk into—and what would we want them to experience instead?

# CHAPTER 8

# The Case for Purpose

*Culture eats strategy for breakfast.*
—Peter Drucker

## Introduction: From Trust to Purpose

In Chapter 7, we explored how psychological safety and trust form the foundation for collective leadership. When teams feel safe to speak candidly and challenge ideas without fear, they build resilience and adaptability. Yet trust alone doesn't answer a deeper question: *Why are we here together at all?*

When the daily pressures of deliverables, deadlines, and competing priorities set in, it's easy to slip into a purely transactional mindset. People do their jobs because they must. They deliver because it's expected. But teams that operate only on transactional energy rarely sustain high performance or fulfillment over time.

Purpose is what transforms a collection of competent individuals into something more—a cohesive, motivated group committed to a shared vision. It is the force that keeps people moving forward when circumstances become uncertain or uncomfortable.

Purpose is not a slogan on the wall or a polished paragraph in a corporate brochure. It is the lived, authentic answer to three questions:

1. Why do we exist?
2. How do we behave together?
3. What impact are we committed to making?

This chapter is about helping you and your team answer these questions honestly. It will offer a structured process for clarifying your purpose, anchoring your values, and crafting a vision and mission that people believe in, not because they were told to, but because they feel it resonates.

## The Power of Purpose in Uncertain Times

In stable environments, teams can survive without a clear purpose. But in times of volatility—shifting markets, disruptive technology, and cultural change—purpose becomes essential. It guides decision-making, fuels engagement, and enables faster adaptation.[33]

Consider the healthcare team I worked with during the early months of the COVID-19 pandemic. For years, their unspoken purpose had been to deliver efficient patient care while meeting operational targets. When the crisis hit, those targets became nearly impossible to meet. Early in the pandemic, they gathered (virtually) to ask, *"What matters most right now?"*

Their answer was simple: **We are here to protect and reassure people in a time of fear.** That purpose didn't change the challenges, but it did change their mindset. Decisions that once felt difficult became clearer. Trade-offs became more tolerable. Burnout, while still present, was mitigated by the knowledge that their work mattered.

Purpose is the antidote to chaos because it gives people a compass. When everything else feels unstable, purpose is the anchor that says, *"This is why we show up."*

## The Dangers of Hollow Purpose

It's important to be clear: declaring a purpose statement does not mean you have a purpose-driven culture. In fact, a hollow or inauthentic statement can damage credibility more than having no statement at all.[34]

Consider the example of Wells Fargo, which touted customer-centric values while incentivizing employees to open unauthorized accounts. The disconnect between words and actions didn't just create a public relations crisis; it bred cynicism internally. Employees knew the stated values were a façade. Over time, this eroded trust and engagement.

In contrast, organizations that align words and actions, even imperfectly, create cultures of integrity. Employees may not expect perfection, but they do expect honesty. A purpose that is genuinely embraced is imperfectly lived and regularly revisited. It is not a static declaration but a living commitment.

## Why Purpose Matters to Teams

Beyond large-scale examples, purpose has everyday relevance to any team, regardless of industry or size.

1. **Purpose Unites Diverse Motivations.** Teams are collections of people with different life experiences, personal drivers, and career aspirations. Some are motivated by stability, others by growth, and others still by impact. A clear purpose creates a unifying context that transcends individual agendas.

2. **Purpose Informs Decisions.** When teams face ambiguous choices, purpose becomes a decision filter. It helps clarify which opportunities align and which are distractions. A team without purpose can become reactive, chasing every shiny object without coherence.
3. **Purpose Fuels Resilience.** During setbacks, purpose reminds people why perseverance matters. It allows teams to reframe challenges as opportunities to live their values more fully.
4. **Purpose Supports Accountability.** When everyone understands the "why," accountability becomes less about compliance and more about commitment. People hold themselves and each other to a higher standard because they care about the impact they have.

## Introducing the Golden Circle

One of the most helpful frameworks for articulating purpose is Simon Sinek's **Golden Circle Model**, which invites teams to define three dimensions:

- **Why:** The core purpose or belief that inspires you.
- **How:** The values and guiding principles that shape how you work.
- **What:** The tangible products, services, or outcomes you deliver.[35]

When teams start with "why," they create a sense of shared meaning that informs everything else. Sinek argues that people don't buy what you do; they buy why you do it.[36] While this insight is often applied to branding and marketing, it's equally powerful internally. When employees understand and believe in the "why," they bring more creativity, ownership, and energy to their work.

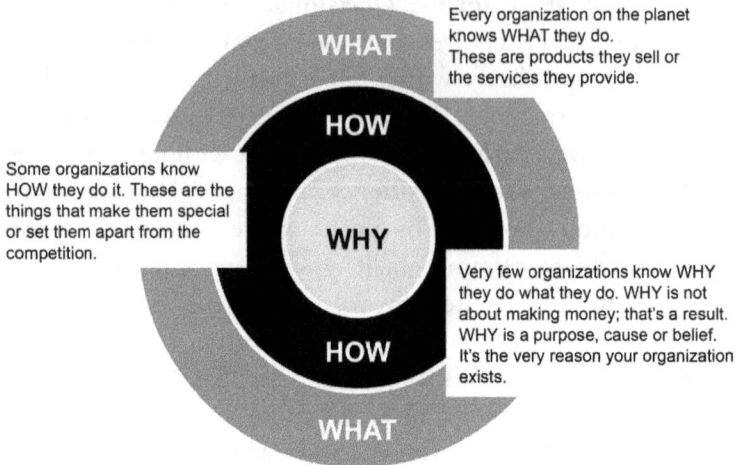

**WHAT**

Every organization on the planet knows WHAT they do. These are products they sell or the services they provide.

**HOW**

Some organizations know HOW they do it. These are the things that make them special or set them apart from the competition.

**WHY**

Very few organizations know WHY they do what they do. WHY is not about making money; that's a result. WHY is a purpose, cause or belief. It's the very reason your organization exists.

**HOW**

**WHAT**

Figure 8.1: The Golden Circle Model

## Reflection: Checking for Authenticity

Before you proceed with defining your team's purpose, it's worth pausing to ask:

- Are we willing to be honest about why we exist?
- Are we prepared to align our behaviors with what we say matters?
- What evidence will we look for that our purpose is being lived, not just stated?

These questions can feel uncomfortable, but they are essential. An authentic purpose doesn't emerge from consensus alone—it requires candor, sometimes confrontation, and a commitment to ongoing practice.

## Defining Values: The Heartbeat of Your Team

Values are more than words you recite in team meetings or print on a poster. They are the shared beliefs that shape decisions, inform behavior, and set the tone for your culture. If your purpose is the compass pointing to your "why," your values are the guideposts showing "how" you will get there together. When values are clear, people know what is expected even when no one is watching. When values are vague or absent, decisions become inconsistent, and trust erodes.

Some teams set out to accomplish a compelling team vision with a goal that is often ten years or more into the future, without acknowledging what they currently value together. I have one question for them: without knowing the current values of the team, it's difficult to think about what we will want to focus on in the future, so what is the purpose of attempting to create a vision and/or mission statement without truly knowing what it is we stand for as a team?

In a recent example with a large organization where Tom and I worked, we asked, "What are your top five values on the team?" After an awkward pause that had everyone looking at each other for an answer, they listed their team values as trustworthiness, integrity, accountability, transparency, and client-centricity.

When asked to define the meaning of each one, there was a deafening silence, as they had almost randomly chosen values they felt they had to state rather than discovering their team's unique values that would unify their commitment. With the challenge set to define them together, they explored deeper meanings, and I noticed their values had shifted over time.

With values that began with integrity morphing into something broader, such as "doing the right thing," they surprised themselves, as this was not among their original responses.

*How could a team just change what they valued? What was the reasoning for the modifications? Did the team make up their initial responses?*

What Tom and I have learned over and over is that teams don't *change* their values; they *uncover* them. The initial answers often reflect what they believe they are *supposed* to say, shaped by corporate language, social pressure, or a desire to look aligned. But once they engage in honest dialogue, shared stories, and real examples of how they want to show up for one another, the *real* values emerge. These aren't invented, they are remembered, clarified, or discovered for the first time.

When working with successful teams, we have noticed that many have not yet had a conversation about values, or, in some cases, the leader has come in and imposed their personal value system. That rarely works, because values that are declared but not co-created have no emotional weight or practical resonance. Teams adopt what they help define, and they commit to what reflects their lived experience, not inherited language. That is the power of doing this work together as a cohesive team.

## Why Values Matter

Consider two product teams working under tight deadlines. One values transparency, so when problems arise, team members flag them early. The other values individual heroics, so people hide issues until the last minute. The first team resolves setbacks faster and with less drama. The second operates in cycles of crisis and blame.

Values don't just live in statements; they live in choices. They are revealed when trade-offs are required.

## Questions to Surface Real Values

When you start defining values as a team, don't begin with aspirational slogans. Start with observation. Here are three questions to explore together:

1. **What behaviors earn respect here?** Think of moments when someone gained credibility. What did they do?
2. **What behaviors damage trust?** Reflect on times when confidence in a teammate was lost. Why?
3. **When we are at our best, what do we consistently demonstrate?** Describe real examples, not ideals.

This reflection grounds your values in lived experience rather than corporate jargon.

## Case Example: Values Discovery Session

A regional wealth management team I worked with was struggling to articulate its values. Everyone agreed they wanted to be "client-focused," but the phrase meant different things to each person.

In a facilitated session, we asked them to tell stories of moments when they felt most proud of their work. Patterns emerged:

- Speaking uncomfortable truths to clients instead of telling them what they wanted to hear.
- Collaborating across roles without worrying about credit.
- Taking ownership when mistakes happen rather than deflecting blame.

Out of those stories came three core values:

1. Courageous Candor
2. Collective Accountability
3. Service Without Ego

These values felt authentic because they were rooted in experience, not marketing language. What is being expressed here is that it is valuable to do some pre-work before the team shows up to collaborate, so that these meetings can be productive in hearing each other's thoughts and gaining a higher level of engagement.

Once the team members are all on the same page and confident in what the team stands for, they can work toward building team cohesion. This will open the door to direction and clarity in areas like effective decision making, time management, and how to support one another while achieving individual goals and those that support the team.

## From Words to Behaviors

Naming values is only the first step. To make them real, define what each value looks like in action.

### Example

**Value:** Courageous Candor

### Behavioral Indicators

- Sharing observations even when they may be unpopular.
- Offering constructive feedback regularly.
- Asking for feedback on your own performance.

This clarity helps everyone align expectations.

## Crafting a Mission Statement: Your Present Focus

While values define how you behave, a mission statement defines what you do and for whom you do it right now. It describes your core purpose in action.

### Mission vs. Vision

- **Mission:** What you commit to doing every day.
- **Vision:** The aspirational future you hope to create.

Think of the mission as your current lane, and the vision as your destination on the horizon.

### Characteristics of a Strong Mission Statement

**Clear:** Avoid jargon or abstract language.
**Specific:** Define who you serve and what you deliver.
**Inspiring:** Reflect on why the work matters.
**Action-Oriented:** Use active verbs.

An effective mission statement can add value to your organization simply because it is a commitment to team members and to external partners, customers, and prospects you'll want to serve moving forward. This commitment streamlines the team's time management, communication, and execution on all future projects. In this situation, I had the team start by visualizing a three- to five-year timeline, prompting them to address the following criteria.

A mission statement does not have to be a repackaged, meaningless slogan. For example, when working as a leadership coach at Wells Fargo Advisors, our Mission Statement was plastered on the cafeteria walls, touted in our literature, and preached to us by our CEO and other C-suite leaders. In reality, we learned in 2016 that our organization committed fraud at the highest level, and we were the first organization to be put under a growth ban by the Federal Reserve.

At times, organizations create these mission statements in some back room, which can feel like a made-up, meaningless slogan dreamed up by a corporate C-suite team or repackaged from some leadership book they just read. Whether it is a large organization or a smaller team, Tom and I can't stress enough the importance of having stakeholders involved in creating and aligning your culture of purpose.

## Examples of Strong Mission Statements

**Patagonia:** *We're in business to save our home planet.*
**Warby Parker:** *To offer designer eyewear at a revolutionary price, while leading the way for socially conscious businesses.*
**Teach For America:** *To enlist, develop, and mobilize as many as possible of our nation's most promising future leaders to grow and strengthen the movement for educational equity and excellence.*

Each statement is memorable, clear, and anchored in purpose.

## Exercise: Crafting Your Mission Statement

Use these questions to begin:

- Who do we serve?
- What do we deliver that makes a meaningful difference?
- How do we deliver it differently or better?
- Why does this work matter now?

## Case Story: Mission Statement Alignment

A midsize architecture firm had grown quickly, expanding into new regions and market segments. But as they grew, their purpose became blurred. Project managers were making decisions in silos, and brand identity began to erode.

During a leadership retreat, the partners shared their individual visions. While each had a different perspective, a theme emerged: a commitment to creating spaces that improve human connection.

From this, they drafted a new mission statement:

> *"We design environments that inspire belonging and bring people together."*

When they shared this with employees, feedback was immediate: *"This feels like us."*

## Coaching Prompts for Leaders

Before you finalize any mission statement, ask yourself:

- Could a competitor say the same thing?
- Would a new employee feel clarity reading this?
- Does it feel true to our culture and aspirations?

A mission statement that feels too safe often ends up too generic.

## Pitfalls to Avoid

**Creating by Committee:** While input matters, wordsmithing by large groups dilutes clarity.

**Aspirational Overload:** Statements that are too lofty feel disconnected from daily work.

**Infrequent Relevance:** If no one references the mission in meetings or decisions, it's time to revisit.

## Transition to Vision

With your mission defined, you set the stage for the next step: crafting an inspiring vision that galvanizes the team for the future. In the following section, we'll explore how to bring this aspirational narrative to life. One of the most important things you can do as a team is to gather insights, perspectives, and experiences from all team members, so much so that they become ingrained in the entire team and are effortlessly communicated to internal and external stakeholders.

Building a culture of purpose requires aligning all components with a long-term, forward-looking strategy. From here, the team can achieve focus, clarity, and intentionality in their daily actions. Let's examine a few examples from other Fortune 500 organizations' vision-statements, similar to our approach with mission statements.

- **Nike:** To bring inspiration and innovation to every athlete in the world.
- **Southwest:** To become the world's most loved, most flown, and most profitable airline.
- **Google:** To provide access to the world's information in one click.
- **Visa:** To uplift everyone, everywhere by being the best way to pay and be paid.

## Why Vision Matters

A clear vision does more than describe an aspirational future; it provides direction, coherence, and a shared understanding of what the team is working toward. Without a compelling vision to anchor decisions, even highly capable teams can become reactive, unfocused, or fragmented in their efforts. Research on organizational growth and development reinforces this idea: mission and vision statements serve as unifying mechanisms that align behavior, guide strategy, and help teams navigate complexity with purpose and clarity.[37]

When vision is absent or vague, people work hard but not necessarily in the same direction. Decisions become inconsistent. Momentum stalls. But when a vision is clearly defined and genuinely embraced, it energizes the team. It links today's actions to tomorrow's aspirations and creates the sense that everyone is contributing to something bigger than themselves. Vision becomes more than words; it becomes the team's north star.

## Crafting a Vision Statement: Your Aspirational North Star

While your mission defines what you do today, your vision describes the future you aspire to create. A strong vision statement provides a unifying destination that guides decisions, inspires innovation, and sustains momentum during challenges.

### What Makes a Compelling Vision?

A vision should be:

1. **Aspirational:** It stretches the imagination beyond current realities.
2. **Clear:** It is simple enough for everyone to remember.

3. **Purpose-Driven:** It reflects why your work matters.
4. **Measurable:** Even if ambitious, it should give clues about what progress looks like.

## Exercise: Envisioning Your Future

Gather your team and ask these questions:

- If we were wildly successful in 5–10 years, what would be true?
- What impact would we be most proud of?
- What would our stakeholders—clients, colleagues, community—say about us?
- What would we be doing differently from today?

Encourage imaginative thinking before refining language.

## Case Story: The Nonprofit Vision

I worked with a nonprofit tackling food insecurity. Their original vision was vague: *"To make a difference in hunger."*

Through facilitated dialogue, the team realized their real aspiration was to empower communities to achieve self-sufficiency. After several iterations, they landed on: *"A future where every community has the resources and confidence to end hunger locally."*

This clarity not only energized staff but also attracted new funders who shared that aspiration. The vision statement is distinct because it has the potential to create an emotional connection, with purpose and intent, to the organization and those it will serve. The core focus is clear and concise and aligns with the mission statement, strategies, and values that represent the team's daily actions.

### Coaching Prompts

Before finalizing a vision statement, ask:

- Does this excite us?
- Could any organization claim this, or does it feel uniquely ours?
- Is it clear enough that everyone can repeat it without notes?

## Bringing Vision and Mission Together

When you read your mission and vision side by side, they should feel complementary:

**Mission:** What we do every day.
**Vision:** The future our work makes possible.

### Example

**Mission:** To connect people with meaningful work opportunities.
**Vision:** A world where everyone can access work that sustains and inspires them.

# Setting Strategy: From Aspiration to Action

Once your purpose, values, mission, and vision are clear, you must translate them into a strategy, the bridge between intention and execution.

**Strategy answers three questions:**

1. Where will we focus?
2. How will we succeed?
3. What will we say no to?

Without a strategy, purpose remains an inspiring idea that never gains traction.

**Three Elements of Strategy**

1. **Priorities:** What are the three to five things we must do exceptionally well?
2. **Capabilities:** What strengths will we leverage?
3. **Measures:** How will we track progress?

## Case Example: Strategic Focus in Action

A mid-sized marketing firm wanted to become known for purpose-driven campaigns. Their leadership team clarified their mission and vision, then identified three strategic priorities:

- Build a portfolio of nonprofit and social enterprise clients.
- Develop storytelling capabilities rooted in authenticity.
- Invest in team training to align values with practice.

Each priority had clear measures, such as the percentage of revenue from impact clients and client satisfaction scores. This clarity empowered every team member to make decisions aligned with purpose.

To clarify your strategy, create a simple canvas. For example:

## Table 8.1: Practical Exercise: Strategy Canvas

| Focus Area | Why It Matters | How We Win | What We Won't Do | Measures |
|---|---|---|---|---|
| Client Experience | Drives retention and referrals | Personalized service and proactive communication | Rely solely on transactional touchpoints | NPS score, renewal rates |

Review and update quarterly to stay relevant.

### Coaching Questions for Leaders

- What are we saying no to in order to stay true to our strategy?
- Where might we be spreading ourselves too thin?
- How will we communicate priorities so everyone feels ownership?

### Pitfalls to Avoid

1. **Overcomplexity:** Strategy should be easy to explain.
2. **Lack of trade-offs:** If everything is a priority, nothing is.
3. **Static plans:** Strategy must evolve as your environment changes.

## Visual Reinforcement

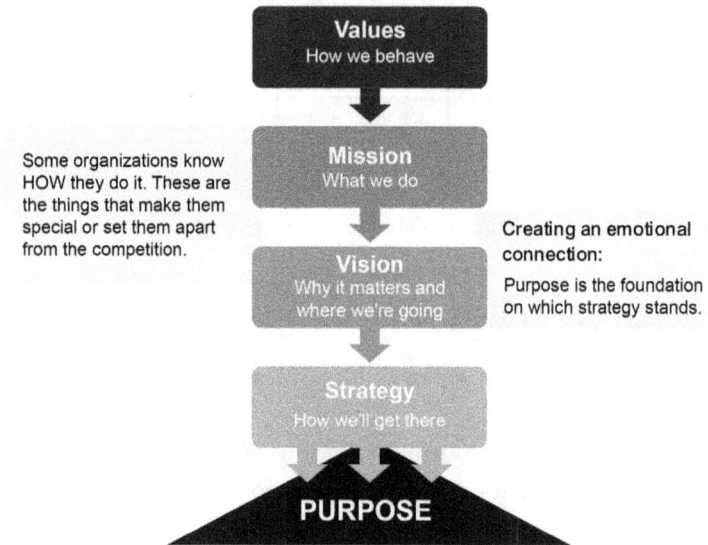

**Values**
How we behave

**Mission**
What we do

**Vision**
Why it matters and
where we're going

**Strategy**
How we'll get there

**PURPOSE**

Some organizations know
HOW they do it. These are
the things that make them
special or set them apart
from the competition.

Creating an emotional
connection:

Purpose is the foundation
on which strategy stands.

Figure 8.2: Values–Mission–Vision–Strategy Flow

## Transition to Activation

Once you have clarity on purpose and strategy, the real work
begins: activating it consistently. In the next section, we'll
explore how to embed purpose in daily practices, rituals, and
conversations so it doesn't remain an unused document but
becomes a living part of your culture.

# Activating Purpose: From Words to Action

Crafting a purpose statement, defining values, and clarifying
mission and vision are foundational steps. But even the most

beautifully written declarations are inert if they live only in a slide deck. Activation is the process of translating purpose into everyday behaviors, rituals, and systems, so it becomes part of how the team works.

## The Purpose Activation Cycle

When teams succeed at activating purpose, they follow a consistent cycle.

- **Communicate.** They articulate purpose often and in different formats.
- **Embed.** They integrate purpose into systems and processes.
- **Model.** Leaders demonstrate purpose-driven behaviors.
- **Reinforce.** They celebrate examples and correct misalignments.

Let's explore each in turn.

### *1. Communicate Purpose Frequently*

Teams often assume people remember what was said in the kickoff or retreat. In reality, messages fade without repetition. Consider the "rule of seven," which suggests people need to hear something at least seven times in different ways to internalize it.

Ways to reinforce purpose include:

- Storytelling in all-hands meetings.
- Visual reminders in shared spaces.
- Including purpose language in onboarding materials.
- Referencing purpose explicitly in decision-making.

**Example**

A technology startup Tom coached was going through their day-to-day task, completing them as "check the box" exercises—minimal hints of collaboration, prioritization, or even supporting each other. They did not focus on what was important or on the connection between them. They were not aligned with what they were there to accomplish.

Tom coached them to place their purpose statement in every sprint planning deck. When evaluating backlog items, they asked, "Does this move us closer to our vision?" Over time, this practice created a culture where purpose wasn't abstract; it was part of every conversation. Simply having a consistent conversation about whether we are on track with our purpose sparks curiosity in the team to shift their mindset and actions, ultimately driving results that focus on what truly matters.

## 2. Embed Purpose in Systems

If you want purpose to feel real, you must bake it into the way you operate.

**Examples of embedding**

- **Performance reviews:** Tie evaluation criteria to values-based behaviors.
- **Hiring processes:** Assess candidates' alignment with purpose.
- **Resource allocation:** Prioritize projects that advance the vision.
- **Recognition programs:** Celebrate contributions that exemplify purpose.

## Case Story: Purpose-Based Recognition

One team I have had the honor of coaching began to implement a consistent recognition program that was not focused on revenue or profitability. They focused on actions that aligned with their vision, mission, and values. Each team member would anonymously nominate another team member for something they witnessed them do that supported their culture.

This financial services firm created what they titled "Living Our Purpose" awards, which were communicated in person each quarter. At first, it felt like just another forced program. However, when the team implemented this with energy and authenticity, it became a source of pride and storytelling. New employees cited it as evidence that purpose mattered beyond slogans. Customer survey scores went up. Assets per client went up. Introductions to friends, family members, and co-workers went up.

Recall the *Efficient Frontier of Teaming*, focusing on authenticity and engagement. These levers were hard at work with the creativity of this team supporting their ability to reach the heights of an Empowered Team.

## 3. Model Purpose as Leaders

People watch leaders closely for clues about what really matters. When leaders embody purpose, it becomes credible. When leaders contradict stated values, cynicism grows.

### Example

If a leader claims transparency is a core value but hoards information, the inconsistency is obvious. Conversely, when a leader admits mistakes and shares learning openly, it sends a powerful signal that transparency is not just tolerated but expected.

## Coaching Prompts

Ask yourself:

- Where do my actions align with our purpose?
- Where do they fall short?
- What is one small behavior I can change this week to better model our values?

## 4. Reinforce Purpose Consistently

Over time, teams drift from stated values. Regularly bringing purpose back into the conversation prevents this drift.

### Simple Reinforcement Tactics

- **Purpose retrospectives:** Once per quarter, discuss: What decisions or behaviors have reinforced our purpose? What has eroded it?
- **Spotlighting stories:** Begin meetings by sharing examples of purpose in action.
- **Feedback loops:** Invite colleagues to share when they see purpose alignment or misalignment.

### Case Story: Quarterly Purpose Retrospectives

A regional healthcare organization holds a quarterly purpose retrospective where teams reflect on successes and failures through the lens of their mission. One manager shared that this ritual created "a safe space to name the gap between aspiration and reality." Over time, these reflections became a catalyst for continuous improvement.

This is a team where failure was seen as negative rather than as a learning opportunity rooted in a growth mindset.

Carolyn Dweck has done tremendous work in this space. Tom and I both recommend her book *Mindset,* where she discusses the differences between someone with a fixed mindset who feels that their intelligence is fixed versus someone with a growth mindset who approaches failures with curiosity to develop.[38]

Providing time for your team to reflect openly and objectively allows you to understand where they can grow and where they can invest their time to continually develop and reach their full potential. It's data that tells a story (Desimone, 2024).[39] Read it consistently and pivot where needed.

## Sustaining Purpose Over Time

Purpose activation is not a project with an end date—it's an ongoing discipline.

Here are four strategies to sustain alignment:

1. **Integrate Into Onboarding.** Introduce purpose and values to new hires from day one. Pair them with mentors who model alignment.
2. **Embed in Decision-Making.** Use purpose as a filter for priorities. Ask, "Does this decision move us toward our vision?"
3. **Adapt as You Grow.** Periodically revisit your purpose to ensure relevance. Growth brings new challenges that may require refining statements or practices.
4. **Celebrate Progress.** Recognize milestones and individuals who exemplify purpose. Reinforcement fuels commitment.

**Pitfalls to Avoid**

- **Purpose Fatigue:** Repeating the same language without fresh stories can breed disengagement.
- **Overreliance on Leaders:** If purpose lives only in the mouths of executives, it never becomes collective.
- **Misalignment with Incentives:** If bonuses reward behavior that contradicts values, purpose becomes hollow.

# Conclusion: A Culture Worth Building

Organizations around the globe create subcultures that prioritize ownership, accountability, and responsibility. This kind of environment creates a purposeful workday, enabling teams to build cohesion and operate more effectively together. When a team simply goes through the motions and lacks meaning behind their daily tasks, they underperform and become transactional.

Purpose is more than a statement; it is the foundation of culture, the lens for decisions, and the fuel for resilience. Teams that commit to purpose don't just perform better; they create environments where people feel their work matters. When individuals feel connected to something bigger, they bring their energy, creativity, and courage to every challenge.

As you move forward, remember that purpose is not static. It evolves as your team grows. Revisit it regularly, challenge it honestly, and let it guide you toward the culture you aspire to build. In the next chapter, we'll explore how accountability structures support this work—so your purpose is not just inspiration, but a commitment you uphold together.

## Taking Action

- Define your top five values.
- Develop a compelling mission statement.
- Craft a vision statement for the future.
- Define strategies to support your team's success.

# CHAPTER 9

# Measuring the Right Things

*If you cannot measure it, you cannot improve it.*
—Lord Kelvin

## Opening Bridge: From Purpose to Performance

In Chapter 8, we explored how purpose fuels direction, energy, and cohesion within teams. Purpose answers the *why* and the deeper reason behind the work. But purpose alone doesn't guarantee progress. Without the right measurements, even the most inspired teams can drift off course.

Clarity of mission must be matched by clarity of metrics. What gets measured sends a message: this is what we value, and this is how we define progress. As coaches, Tom and I often remind leaders: your metrics are your *real priorities*, whether you say them out loud or not. Peter Drucker famously said, "What gets measured gets managed." But Lord Kelvin takes it one step further: "When you can measure what you are speaking about and express it in numbers, you know something about it; but when you cannot express it in numbers, your knowledge is of a meagre and unsatisfactory kind."

This chapter is about building a *measurement operating system* that reflects what matters most—and keeps your team aligned, energized, and executing at a high level.

## Why Measurement Matters to Engagement and Execution

We have coached dozens of teams that start the year with great enthusiasm. They hold retreats, brainstorm big goals, and even write vision statements on glossy posters. Something interesting happens, then by March or April, the energy fades. The goals grow fuzzy, and worse, there's no clear sense of how to know whether they're on track or not. What's missing isn't motivation; it's measurement to understand not only how we are performing but where we can improve.

Measurement and goal tracking, although sometimes overlooked, can be among the most valuable tools for building team alignment and achieving both organizational and individual goals. Creating priorities that can be measured provides a roadmap that prevents employees from getting derailed and losing consistency, ultimately preventing them from maintaining focus on their time, energy, and skills. Without this roadmap, employees will lack clear priorities and thorough communication, resulting in a blurred sense of where they need to focus to improve.

In his book *The 7 Habits of Highly Effective People*, author Stephen Covey breaks down the seven habits and guides readers with questions and statements.[40] I've seen how these habits create a framework that gives the team permission to focus on important priorities rather than the urgency of day-to-day tasks, which can overwhelm everyone.

## The Role of Measurement in Momentum

Research confirms this: teams that track progress consistently outperform those that don't. A meta-analysis of 138 studies found that goal setting combined with feedback led to significantly higher performance than goal setting alone.[41] Measurement fuels feedback, which in turn reinforces effort. Research shows that the experience of making visible progress, even through small wins, is one of the strongest drivers of engagement, motivation, and sustained performance at work.[42]

In other words, metrics don't just inform, they *motivate*. When team members can see progress in real time, they adjust, self-correct, and stay engaged. Now we see the connection: engagement is at its lowest in over a decade in the United States and across the globe.[43] Teams that struggle to build out Key Performance Indicators (KPIs), identify rocks, and understand how to review consistently show that their team members lose focus. There is a connection here that is screaming for attention. Most of the time, teams and leaders know they need to build out success measures, track them, and discuss them. However, it's shocking how often this gets left off the table or becomes an occasional check-in with little commitment to next steps for improvement.

## Measurement as Alignment

Measurement does more than energize. It aligns. Think of your team like a rowing crew. If each member is pulling at a different rhythm, or worse, rowing in a different direction, then you don't get far. I live right outside a rowing canal in Belmont Shores, CA, and when things are off, the rowing coach is not shy about correcting the faults. Measurement is the coxswain's cadence. It keeps everyone in sync, focused on the shared destination.

When Tom and I are coaching teams through a measurement reset, I often ask the leadership group these questions:

- "What are the five most important outcomes this team is responsible for?"
- "If we got to the end of the year and accomplished just three things, what would they be?"
- "How do you currently measure those things—if at all?"
- "Where is your time going right now? Do your hours reflect your priorities?"
- "What gets talked about every week? Are those the right conversations?"

These questions help uncover misalignments. Often, the stated goals don't match the metrics. Or the metrics exist—but they're buried in dashboards no one reads. Sometimes teams measure outputs they can't control rather than activities they can influence.

## The Covey Lens: Beginning with the End in Mind

Stephen Covey's second habit is "Begin with the end in mind," which is foundational here.[44] If your team doesn't know what success looks like, how can they build toward it? More than 80 percent of the teams we have worked with don't revisit their strategic goals regularly. They spend time in meetings, they respond to urgent issues, but they don't take time to zoom out and ask: Are we moving the needle?

The cost of this? Burnout, misalignment, and a culture that mistakes activity for progress. By contrast, teams that operate at an optimal performance level make metrics part of the rhythm. They track what matters and review it often to recognize success and learn from gaps. They keep the scoreboard visible.

As we've discussed, without a clear definition of what success looks like, it makes it extremely difficult for teams to understand where they need to focus their time and attention, what they are doing that is playing to their strengths, and where can they spend time to continually develop their skills in areas of opportunity that are causing them to lag in their collective results.

## The Role of Measurement in Team Performance

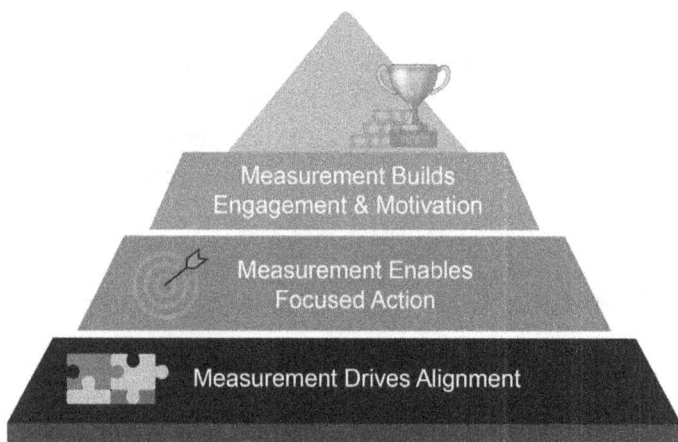

Figure 9.1: The Role of Measurement in Team Performance

## Coaching Reflection Prompt

**Ask your team:**

- "What did we set out to accomplish as a team this year?" "What are we measuring right now? And does it actually reflect what matters most?"

- "What areas of strength are contributing to success each month?"
- "How can we take specific action steps to develop opportunities that will improve our collective results?"

## When Measurements Don't Line Up: A Case of Misalignment

A few years ago, I was coaching a leadership team at a fast-growing telecommunications company called Crown Castle. Their mission was bold: improve infrastructure timelines for deploying 5G technology across the US. Yet despite all the talent in the room, something was off.

They had strong engineering. Solid project managers. Clear market demand, but their major carrier clients were frustrated. They kept asking, "Why do you keep missing dates?" So, we whiteboarded the full process, from sales to engineering, permitting, construction, and final activation. Here's what we found:

- The **sales team** promised clients a **90-day install timeline.**
- The **permitting team** realistically needed **120 days**.
- The **construction team** said, "We can't even mobilize until day 150."
- And **operations**? They weren't even looped in until permits were cleared.

Within this highly matrixed organization, each team had its own timeline and its own success metrics. Sales got credit for signed deals. Permitting measured permit volume. Construction celebrated project closeouts. However, no one was measuring **end-to-end delivery**. To take things even further, the blame game was played daily between departments like an adult version of duck-duck-goose. Instead of communicating the collective deadlines, requirements, and customer demands, each department did its own thing.

Sales reps promised 90-day delivery for equipment installation, even though obtaining construction permits would take 180 days. The construction team would separately inform the customer that the project would take 250 days. Then the engineering department would shuffle in, trying to figure out what plans they even needed to map out. This caused not only customer frustration but also significant upset and disengagement among team members. Everyone was passing the blame around instead of taking ownership and communicating the team's metrics, not the silos.

## The Danger of Siloed Metrics

This isn't unique to Crown Castle. Many organizations suffer from the same pattern. Each department optimizes for its own scoreboard, unintentionally sabotaging the bigger goal.

Researchers call this the **"suboptimization trap,"** which is when one part of the system improves at the expense of the whole.[45] In team coaching, we have seen it lead to missed targets, broken trust, and finger-pointing that wastes valuable time and morale.

A global study of C-level executives found that 75 percent admit they do not have a very high level of trust in their data, underscoring how fragile data confidence can be and how easily fragmented metrics can erode alignment.[46]

## The Misalignment Path

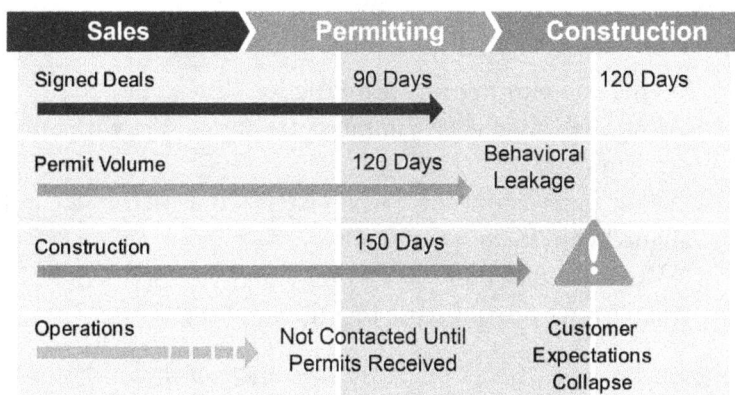

| Sales | Permitting | Construction |
|---|---|---|
| Signed Deals | 90 Days | 120 Days |
| Permit Volume | 120 Days | Behavioral Leakage |
| Construction | 150 Days | ⚠ |
| Operations | Not Contacted Until Permits Received | Customer Expectations Collapse |

Without shared milestones, each function wins alone—and the customer loses.

**Figure 9.2: The Misalignment Path**

## Coaching Insight: Cascade and Integrate

The fix wasn't to tell sales to stop selling. It was to **co-create a shared measurement system**. We built a common milestone map with clear phase gates. Then we adjusted sales goals to align with realistic delivery timelines. Permitting and construction metrics were updated to reflect client-facing outcomes rather than just internal throughput.

The change didn't happen overnight. But six months later, the delivery timelines dropped by 22 percent, and client satisfaction scores jumped. Your team might not need more metrics. It needs the **right, shared ones** that tell the *full story* and serve to set the entire team up for success to shine.

*Coaching Reflection Prompt*

**Ask your team:**

> "Where do our metrics create friction instead of flow?"
> "How often should we communicate our metrics with other departments?"
> "What steps can we take when we feel our metrics are not aligned with fueling our results?"
> "When we feel there is an omission of a success metric, what can we do to discuss together?"

# Define Your Rocks: What Matters Most

Imagine trying to pack for a cross-country move, only to find you've filled your boxes with socks and books, leaving no room for the essentials. That's how many teams approach their calendars. They fill their weeks with emails, meetings, and tasks that feel urgent but aren't aligned to what matters most. It's almost as if they create the "aura" of being busy without much in terms of results.

In coaching, we call this the "rocks vs. sand" problem. The metaphor, popularized by Stephen Covey and later adapted in leadership and time-management workshops, is simple but profound:

> "If you don't put the big rocks in first, you'll never get them in at all."[47]

## The Rocks and Sand Capacity Jar

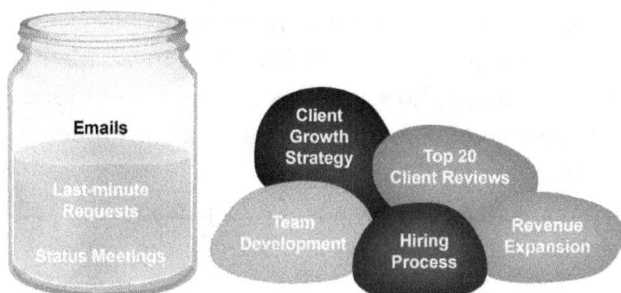

If you don't prioritize the essentials, they'll get crowded out by noise.

**Figure 9.3: The Rocks and Sand Capacity Jar**

## What Are Your Rocks?

Your Rocks are your non-negotiables—the three to five key strategic priorities that, if completed, would make the year a success. This focus on a small number of wildly important priorities mirrors what execution research consistently shows: teams that narrow their attention and track a few critical goals execute more effectively than those that try to pursue everything at once.[48] In my work with wealth advisory teams, we often begin by asking:

- "What are your five Rocks for this quarter?"
- "What would success *look like* and *feel like* if these were complete?"
- "Who owns each rock?"
- "How often do we talk about them as a team?"

When applying this concept with leaders, I always start with one question: What are the top five priority areas you need to spend consistent time in to drive results? When I posed this question to a large wealth advisory team, they had already been considered successful. This proves that a team doesn't have to be broken just because they haven't had this conversation yet. It's simply a testament to how all teams have opportunities to grow, and this happened to be one of their big opportunities.

In one example, a senior partner of a 25-person wealth advisory team shared their draft of top priorities for the quarter:

1. Onboard a new Associate Advisor and define their success plan
2. Review and segment all clients using the new service matrix
3. Launch three client education events tied to market insights
4. Refine the team's investment philosophy and publish it internally
5. Convert $25M to revenue in new business pipeline

Each Rock was assigned an owner and a weekly check-in cadence. These weren't just dreams; they became shared commitments. When you look back at the Rocks this team created, you see areas that gave them energy and increased their engagement in their roles, the team, and the clients they supported.

Putting the Rocks in place as a team helps build out the blueprint that will lead to success for everyone involved, while giving them permission to dedicate their time to certain areas. From there, they can learn to protect that time so nothing becomes urgent and stressful, a situation many teams fall prey to without even realizing it.

## Beware the Sand

Here's the challenge: If you don't consciously define your Rocks, *sand* will fill your jar. In this example with the wealth advisory team, the sand includes:

- Ad-hoc client calls
- Internal status meetings with no decisions
- Low-value compliance tasks that others could own
- Busywork that feels productive but isn't tied to results

When teams bring this metaphor to life visually, whether on a whiteboard, mural, or digital dashboard, it changes how they spend their time. Suddenly, they're not just working hard; they're working with *intent*. In addition, teams that initially claim they are "at capacity," which is one of my triggers, can take an objective look at whether they are busy or doing busy work.

Tom and I can't stress enough how important it is that the team is aligned with what they are called upon to accomplish. Not building out a roadmap just becomes guesswork, and instead of trying to take a road trip to Lake Tahoe, you suddenly end up in Tacoma. We need to stop the silliness and, as organizations, teams, and individuals, find a way to track our performance so it gives us insight, not becomes an accusatory conversation. When I discuss accusatory conversation instead of reviewing and discussing our metrics, it becomes a competition where fingers point. "I'm hitting my individual Rocks, you're not, what's wrong with you?"

Teams that thrive have high levels of engagement and authenticity among their members, building a roadmap to reach the destination as a collective, so everyone can enjoy skiing on the slopes in Tahoe, rather than whatever would occur in Tacoma.

## Research Insight

A recent McKinsey report found that executives spend more than 50 percent of their time on non-strategic tasks, yet high-performing leaders reallocate that time by clearly prioritizing and communicating "must-win" objectives.[49]

Research consistently shows that alignment drives execution speed and organizational performance. For example, a Bain & Company study found that highly aligned organizations outperform others by 58 percent in execution speed.[50] OKRs serve as one mechanism to build this alignment and improve clarity and focus across teams. Popularized by John Doerr, OKRs create a shared language for priorities by linking ambitious objectives with measurable outcomes, reinforcing focus, accountability, and execution discipline.[51]

There are hundreds of additional studies that show the same results. This is not a nice-to-have; it is a must if you and your team want to reach your full potential and deliver results for the organization and for each other.

## Coaching Insight: Don't Choose More than Five

If everything's a priority, nothing is. I coach teams to resist the temptation to overload their Rocks. Five is a stretch goal. Three is often more realistic for small teams. Instead of adding more, define **what done looks like** and revisit those goals weekly. That creates consistency, accountability, and forward movement.

Discuss as a team so everyone can contribute to building ownership across the areas that need to be addressed. Team members will need to collaborate to address time constraints, priorities, and progress measurement. Remember, at this stage, we are just quantifying the time needed so that, later, we can begin crafting the teams' strategies and activities they will implement. Right now, it is important to quantify how much time the team will commit to each rock to support one another.

Prioritizing the team's time is not just about setting goals. It adds substance and focus to each team member's daily tasks, ultimately driving the organization's results. Now that the team is committing to a target of the time needed, they are giving themselves permission to decide where to shift their attention and what is urgent and what can wait. Safeguarding this time and measuring your team members' abilities to stick to their Rock commitments is key. The following inquiries can be made during weekly team meetings to support each other's success toward the team's common goals.

## Coaching Reflection Prompt

**Ask your team:**

> "What are our three to five big Rocks this quarter—and who owns them?"
> "What led to the team's success in focusing on the Rocks?"
> "What specific action steps can we take to spend the needed time in the Rocks?"
> "When did obstacles appear, and how will we discuss and pivot if appropriate?

# Quantify Your Time: The Hidden KPI

When Tom and I work with leaders, one of the first questions we ask isn't about revenue, assets under management, or productivity. It's this: "How do you spend your time?"

There's usually a pause and then a look of realization. Most high-achieving professionals don't track their time, assuming hard work equals the right work. But time, more than money, is your most finite resource, and most teams never measure it.

Research shows that excessive or poorly structured meetings contribute directly to burnout, fatigue, and reduced focus time, as employees with heavier meeting loads report significantly higher exhaustion and significantly less capacity for concentrated work.[52]

Another RescueTime study found that the average knowledge worker spends only 2 hours and 48 minutes per day on focused, high-impact work. The rest is email, context-switching, and low-leverage activity.[53]

## Time Is Strategy

Time isn't just a scheduling issue. It's a **strategy problem**. If your team's calendar doesn't reflect your top goals—your rocks—it means the strategy hasn't truly cascaded. No amount of motivation can fix a calendar built for firefighting. I often share this story during client retreats:

## Story: The StrengthsFinder Surprise

A senior wealth advisor I coached had just completed the CliftonStrengths® assessment. Her top strengths were **Strategic**, **Maximizer**, and **Futuristic**. She was energized by visionary thinking, long-term planning, and creative problem-solving. However, when we reviewed a sample of her weekly calendar, here's what we found:

- 12 client reviews with little prep time
- 8 internal meetings (4 of which were recurring status checks)
- 2 recruiting calls
- 4 hours of email blocks
- 0 hours of strategy, innovation, or team development

Her calendar was working against her wiring, so we built a **Time Audit Dashboard**. We color-coded her calendar:

- Green = Strategic (creative, growth-oriented, proactive)
- Yellow = Necessary (client work, admin reviews)
- Red = Reactive (fire drills, unplanned meetings)

Less than 10 percent of her time was green.

We didn't just look at the calendar. We spent time redesigning it. We created two "Green Zones" each week: one on Tuesday morning, one on Friday afternoon. These were untouchable blocks for strategic thinking, vision planning, and one-on-one mentorship with her team. Six weeks later, her tone had shifted. "I feel like I'm leading again, not just reacting."

## Research Insight

A McKinsey analysis found that in the highest-performing organizations, senior executives spend *at least 50 percent of their time in decision-focused meetings and less than 10 percent in purely reporting or information meetings*, whereas in many other companies the pattern is almost exactly reversed.[54]

## Coaching Insight: Track, Don't Judge

The goal isn't to shame your calendar as much as it is to **illuminate it**. Have your team complete a one-week time audit. Color code it. Then ask:

- "What percentage of your time is spent on growth?"
- "How much of your week feels reactionary?"
- "Are your rocks showing up in your time, or are they just on a slide deck?"

*Coaching Reflection Prompt*

**Ask your team:**

> "If someone audited your calendar for the last 30 days, what would they say your real priorities are?"
> "What would the results look like if all team members were focused on accomplishing their Rocks?"
> "How can we support each other when time is getting away from us?"
> "What is our process to review our time consistently and realign if needed?"

# Meeting Rhythms That Matter

Every team has meetings, although not every team knows *why* they're meeting. We have both coached firms where meetings became rituals, with weekly check-ins that no one looked forward to and daily standups that felt more like status dumps than momentum builders. The problem isn't too many meetings. It's that there are too many *pointless* meetings.

Research shows that executives spend over **23 hours a week in meetings**, and 67 percent of them say these meetings are unproductive or distracting. Unproductive meetings cost US companies an estimated **$37 billion annually**.[55] For teams chasing performance and alignment, the meeting is one of the most under-leveraged tools available. So how do we fix it?

## Story: From Drifting to Driving

A mid-sized marketing firm that Tom and I worked with had grown quickly. They had added team members, upgraded systems, and expanded their client base. But when we did a diagnostic, the number one complaint was surprisingly consistent: *"Our meetings feel like a waste of time."*

Here's what their typical week looked like:

**Monday:** 45-minute team update (no agenda)
**Wednesday:** Ad hoc client strategy discussion
**Thursday:** 1-hour operations sync with overlapping attendees
**Friday:** Random "recap" meeting that often got canceled

No cadence. No structure. No feedback. And no clear owner of meeting effectiveness.

We made one simple commitment: every meeting would serve a *strategic purpose*, with the **agenda and outcomes defined in advance.** Then, we implemented a tiered system of meeting rhythms based on their goals. Research from the University of North Carolina found that teams with clear meeting agendas and defined outcomes complete significantly more follow-up tasks than teams that meet without structure, reinforcing the link between meeting design and execution.[56]

## The Anatomy of a Great Weekly Meeting

Tom coached the leadership team to reimagine their **weekly tactical sync** with this format:

**Quick Wins (5 minutes)** – What's going well?
**KPI Review (10 minutes)** – Are we on or off track?
**Rock Updates (15 minutes)** – What's the status on big goals?
**Stuck Points (10 minutes)** – Where do we need help?
**Action Items & Ownership (5 minutes)** – Who's doing what by when?

Each meeting had a timekeeper, a note-taker, and an outcomes email sent within 24 hours. We also added a rotating "energy check" at the beginning to keep things human. After six weeks, feedback shifted from frustration to focus. "We actually get stuff done in our meetings now," one team member said. "And I leave knowing what I'm supposed to do."

## Research Insight

Teams that follow a structured meeting agenda and regularly review key priorities are **30 percent more likely to report progress on their goals**.[57] Additional research on meeting processes shows that teams with structured agendas and clearly aligned action steps are significantly more likely to complete follow-up items and achieve better outcomes than teams that do not finalize action items.[58]

This shows that meetings are not the enemy; it is actually poor meeting design. When the mindset shifts from "these meetings are meaningless" to "this is the time, we can re-energize together," it sets a tone. The team looks forward to presenting their results so they can be recognized for their success, but more importantly, be supported in areas where they need help.

Stop holding useless meetings and set expectations for the results when everyone shows up prepared and ready to discuss. If your team dreads its meetings, don't just cancel them. **Redesign them.** Shorter meetings with tighter focus and clearer outcomes drive alignment—and give your team time back to execute. The results may shock you with the small tweaks that we listed above.

*Coaching Reflection Prompt*

**Ask your team:**

> "Which of our meetings are actually moving us forward and which ones need to be redesigned or retired?"
> "How can we hold each other accountable to show up to meetings prepared and engaged?"
> "What steps can we take to maximize our time together?"
> "What will we do when a team member shows up unprepared or is not tracking their progress?"

## Bringing It All Together: A Culture of Continuous Measurement

Teams that perform at an optimal level of performance do not treat measurement as a compliance exercise. For them, it is ingrained in their culture. It's how alignment is maintained, accountability is reinforced, and growth becomes visible. However, measurement only works when it's:

**Intentional:** focused on what matters most
**Shared:** visible and understood across the team
**Actionable:** tied to daily and weekly behavior
**Iterative:** regularly revisited and refined

When these four principles are present, measurement becomes a **flywheel**, creating sustained momentum.

## The Measurement Flywheel

*Measurement drives behavior. Behavior reinforces culture. Culture enables results.*

# The Measurement Flywheel

Figure 9.4: The Measurement Flywheel

**Clarity on Goals** → When teams are clear on what success looks like, they stop reacting to noise and start moving with intention.

**Aligned Metrics** → Metrics translate strategy into focus by measuring what the team can influence, not just what gets reported.

**Visible Scoreboards** → When progress is visible, ownership increases and conversations shift from opinions to shared reality.

**Behavioral Adjustment** → The real power of measurement is not tracking results, but using them to adapt behavior in real time.

## Bringing the Measurement Flywheel Together

What makes this flywheel powerful is not any single component. It is the way they work together as a system. Clarity on goals without aligned metrics creates inspiration without traction. Metrics without visibility become background noise. Scoreboards without behavioral adjustment become passive reporting rather than learning. High-performing teams understand that measurement is not a static exercise. It is a living feedback loop that keeps the team honest, focused, and adaptive. When teams revisit this cycle consistently, they stop guessing where to spend their time and start making intentional choices that compound over time.

In our coaching work, this is where the real shift happens. Conversations move from defensiveness to curiosity. From "Are we busy?" to "Are we making progress?" The flywheel creates shared language and shared ownership, both of which are critical. No one person carries the burden of performance alone. The system does. When teams commit to clarity, align what they measure, make progress visible, and adjust behavior together, measurement stops feeling like control and starts functioning as support. When this rhythm is working, teams feel focused and energized. When it breaks down, even subtly, progress begins to stall, alignment frays, and effort increases without a corresponding lift in results.

## Coaching Sidebar: When the Flywheel Breaks Down

Most teams do not fail because they lack effort. They struggle because one part of the measurement flywheel quietly disconnects from the others. Goals are clear, but metrics do not reflect what actually matters. Metrics exist, but no one regularly sees them. Scoreboards are visible, but nothing changes week to week. Or behavior shifts temporarily, only to drift back once urgency fades.

When this happens, teams often default to frustration or blame. Meetings feel repetitive. Accountability feels personal instead of shared. Energy drops, even though everyone is working hard. The coaching move here is not to add more metrics or more meetings. It is to diagnose where the loop broke and rebuild it deliberately. Ask simple questions together. What are we trying to achieve right now? How are we measuring it? Where are we seeing progress or gaps? And what, specifically, are we willing to do differently next week?

When teams learn to repair the flywheel rather than abandon it, measurement becomes a stabilizing force. It brings the conversation back to learning, ownership, and forward movement. That is where teams regain trust in the process and in each other.

## Integration Tools for Teams

To embed a culture of measurement across your team:

> **Start with the Rocks.** Define three to five priorities each quarter
>
> **Create Time Capacity.** Audit and redesign your team calendar
>
> **Align Meeting Cadence.** Weekly tactical syncs with KPIs and accountability
>
> **Build a Scoreboard.** Focus on visibility, ownership, and weekly updates
>
> **Reflect Routinely.** Ask what's working, what's missing, and what needs to evolve

Each step reinforces the next. As alignment grows, so do engagement, performance, and satisfaction.

## Conclusion: Measuring What Matters

If there's one truth Tom and I have learned in decades of leadership coaching, it's this: *You can't manage what you don't measure—and you shouldn't measure what you won't manage.*

Measurement is not about micromanagement. It's about **clarity, focus,** and **shared ownership.** When your team can see the scoreboard, understand the game plan, and own their impact, it creates an environment to unlock real momentum. Leaders don't need more dashboards. They need better conversations about the right numbers, and when those conversations happen consistently, your team shifts from motion to progress and from activity to achievement.

Prioritizing your time is not easy, especially in today's rapidly changing environment with advances in technology, matrixed teams within organizations, and hybrid and remote roles and positions, among other shifts. It is essential for each team member to find creative ways to manage their time so they can be accountable to themselves and their colleagues. Only then can the team reach high-level success.

Identifying both team and individual measures of success will give permission to focus time, attention, and energy on the areas that will drive results while supporting the organization's vision, mission, and values. This also makes it easy to nail down the strategies you'll want to focus on in the future. Quantify the time you need, clarify which KPI's to measure, and meet consistently to develop the ownership and accountability within the team as you build cohesion together through a lens of support rather than judgment.

## Taking Action

### Define Your Rocks

It's the end of the year, and we are celebrating as a team.

- What did you accomplish?
- What are the priorities and responsibilities of the team as contributors to the overall organization's goals?
- How will you know as a team if you are winning together?

### Quantify Your Time

- How much time do we need to dedicate to each priority area to be successful?
- What steps can we take together to protect this time, knowing the result that is at stake?
- How will we track our progress in sticking to our time or adjusting if needed?

### Identifying Your KPI's

- What are our lagging indicators (results) we want to achieve so that we can celebrate our success at the end of the year?
- What are the leading indicators (actions) that we will take to support executing upon our lagging indicators?
- How will we know if we are "winning" this year?
- What does our Team Scoreboard look like?

### Measuring Your Team's Success

- How often will we meet as a team to review our progress on the Team Scoreboard?

- What does our agenda look like in terms of items to review, timing of each area, and next steps, as well as commitments moving forward?
- How will we show up with curiosity and let go of our judgment to ensure these meetings are conducted in a supportive manner for the team's success?

# CHAPTER 10

# Defining How We Work Together

*Individual commitment to a group effort—*
*that is what makes a team work, a company work,*
*a society work, a civilization work.*
—Vince Lombardi

## The Power of a Team Contract

When I walk into a team's workspace, whether it's a boardroom, a bullpen, or a Zoom gallery, there's one silent indicator that tells me more than any KPI report ever could: how they work together.

Some teams move with rhythm. Others move with friction. The difference usually comes down to a shared agreement, or lack thereof, on how they collaborate, communicate, and show up every day. That's where a team contract becomes essential. This is a tool that Tom and I developed to capture commitment to how the team will engage, communicate, and operate at their fullest potential.

A team contract is not a bureaucratic document. It's a living, breathing agreement created by the team, for the team, that defines how members commit to working with each other. It sets the behavioral expectations, cultural standards, and ground rules that elevate teamwork from accidental to intentional.

I once coached a leadership team within a regional wealth management firm that had all the right ingredients: strong individual talent, a clear strategic direction, and loyal clients. But inside the team, meetings were tense. Emails were misinterpreted. Trust was thin, especially under pressure. Their results were stable, but the energy in the room was always one raised eyebrow away from derailing. People hesitated to speak up. Turnover increased. They didn't need another strategic initiative. They needed clarity on how to treat one another.

Over a two-day offsite, we worked through a series of reflective prompts.

- What behaviors build trust here?
- What behaviors erode it?
- How do we resolve conflict?
- How will we communicate under stress?
- What are our shared expectations around follow-through?

The outcome was a simple, one-page "Operating Code." It included statements like: "We speak to one another, not about one another," and "Assume positive intent, then clarify." It wasn't revolutionary, it was transformational. That team moved from high-strain collaboration to open dialogue, humor, and trust. And that's the point: Great team contracts aren't complicated. They're intentional.

Another story from a client with a cross-functional team inside a fast-growing fintech startup comes to mind. This team was smart and ambitious, but constantly stepping on each other's toes. Engineers were frustrated by last-minute product requirements. Marketing felt developers were too reactive. Leaders wanted innovation, but the dysfunction was dragging down results. Instead of launching a "culture initiative," we did something simpler: each department shared its top three frustrations, and we facilitated a conversation to rewrite the norms.

From that emerged their first "How We Work Together" agreement. It addressed timing, tone, conflict, recognition, and decision rights. It started as a Google Doc, but it became their north star. Within six weeks, velocity increased, satisfaction rose, and a long-delayed product milestone was hit.

As Patrick Lencioni writes in *The Five Dysfunctions of a Team*, most teams avoid conflict because they lack trust, and trust breaks down when expectations are ambiguous.[59] A team contract provides the clarity that fuels safety, collaboration, and performance. Research backs this up. Remember that Google's Project Aristotle found that psychological safety, not talent, tenure, or structure, was the number one predictor of high-performing teams.

Amy Edmondson of Harvard defines psychological safety as "a shared belief held by members of a team that the team is safe for interpersonal risk-taking."[60] When behavioral norms are codified in a team contract, teams are more likely to engage in productive conflict, speak openly, and learn faster.

**What a Team Contract Really Does**

**Figure 10.1: The Team Contract**

**A well-crafted team contract does three things:**

1. Defines the specific behaviors that support the team's mission
2. Builds shared accountability without micromanagement
3. Reinforces psychological safety by making expectations explicit

But how is a team contract different from a mission or vision statement?

A team's mission defines *why* it exists. Its vision defines *what* it hopes to achieve. A team contract defines *how* its members will behave along the way.

- Vision = Destination
- Mission = Purpose
- Team Contract = How we treat each other on the journey

Team contracts are especially effective for leadership teams, cross-functional task forces, and fast-growing companies where norms haven't yet stabilized. The key takeaway is that your team already has unspoken behavioral norms, even if you're not aware of them. A team contract brings them to the surface, creating alignment before misalignment costs you trust, time, or talent.

Whether your team is new or seasoned, co-authoring a contract builds ownership and clarity. It sets the tone for a culture where people not only perform but also belong, allowing everyone to contribute to shaping the norms and empowering them to take ownership of the culture.

# Building a Team Contract: From Intention to Agreement

If the chapter so far has made the case for why team contracts matter, this section is about how to actually build one and what it looks like when it works. A team contract isn't something you download and hand out. It's something that must be co-created through open dialogue, mutual reflection, and shared ownership. Without that, it becomes a policy and not a practice.

Let's take a real-world example.

At Merrill Lynch, a senior wealth advisory team I worked with had been growing rapidly, both in team size and client complexity. The partners were highly competent but working in silos. There were misunderstandings about role expectations, responsiveness, and even meeting etiquette. "We assumed we were aligned," one advisor said. "But our assumptions were very wrong."

To reset, we facilitated a structured process to co-author a team contract. They started with questions such as:

- What does great communication look like on this team?
- How will we handle conflict or disagreement?
- What expectations do we have for accountability, follow-through, and recognition?
- What does respect mean to each of us?

Each team member was given the opportunity to share their thoughts and perspectives. This conversation allows everyone to feel they are supporting the design of the culture of the team rather than it being dictated. What Tom and I have found is that if you allow members of your team to sit at the table together and design the culture, they will then own it because they helped to create it.

The Merrill Lynch final contract included principles like:

- Be fully present in meetings and no distractions allowed.
- Clarify priorities before initiating new client requests.
- Acknowledge each other's efforts publicly and privately.
- Address issues directly, not through side conversations.

They called it their "Working Together Agreement." It wasn't framed in legal terms. It was framed in trust. The team saw a measurable shift within 30 days. Meeting attendance improved. Follow-through became more consistent. Collaboration across roles deepened. Clients even noted the difference, as seen when one emailed a partner to say, "Your whole team seems more dialed in."

This outcome isn't unique. A study from MIT's Sloan School of Management found that teams that co-create behavioral norms outperform those with only top-down expectations, particularly on collaboration and innovation metrics.[61]

To reinforce this point, consider a software engineering team at a Fortune 500 healthcare tech firm. They operated in an agile framework but faced frequent sprint interruptions, mostly due to assumptions rather than actual blockers. The product managers assumed developers had the same definition of "urgent." Developers assumed "client requests" were non-negotiable. Tensions rose.

After a three-hour facilitated session, they co-authored a contract titled, "How We Show Up for Each Other." It included a unique clause: "Urgency must be agreed upon by two parties—requestor and executor." This single line reduced unnecessary escalations by over 50 percent. They also defined their own "Responsiveness Matrix," setting norms around Slack, email, and live meetings.

Research by Edmondson and Google's Project Aristotle reinforces that psychological safety increases when behavior standards are explicit, not assumed.[62] Codifying these standards in a team-authored contract builds both clarity and commitment.

## Sidebar: Building Blocks of a Team Contract

Imagine six foundational "blocks," each representing an area to address when building your Contract:

**Building Blocks of a Team Contract**

Figure 10.2: Building Blocks of a Team Contract

1. **Trust**: What builds or breaks trust?
2. **Communication**: How do we share, listen, and respond?
3. **Conflict**: How do we engage when we disagree?

4. **Accountability**: What does follow-through and ownership look like?
5. **Recognition**: How do we celebrate effort, not just outcomes?
6. **Growth**: How do we reflect and improve together?

Each block is supported by prompting questions and behaviors. When used together, these blocks create a strong foundation for shared norms.

## Coach's Corner: How to Facilitate a Team Contract

1. Discover: Ask each member to describe the team at its best and worst.
2. Define: Pull out themes and values from what was shared.
3. Draft: Collaboratively write agreement statements.
4. Debrief: Invite feedback: What's missing? What feels forced?
5. Deploy: Sign the contract. Post it. Review it monthly.

### 10 Questions to Guide the Process

1. What behaviors create energy on this team?
2. What behaviors diminish trust?
3. How do we want to handle disagreement?
4. What does follow-through look like?
5. What are our expectations around responsiveness?
6. What does "respect" mean to us?
7. How do we want to be recognized?
8. What should we stop doing that's holding us back?
9. How do we want to resolve conflict?
10. How do we commit to keeping this agreement alive?

Creating a team contract is not just a tactical move or, as we discussed earlier in this book, a "check the box" exercise. It is a declaration. It is an act of cultural leadership. It takes what's implicit and makes it explicit. It replaces assumptions with clarity and blame with accountability. As Lencioni reminds us, healthy conflict and accountability are impossible without clarity, and clarity begins with shared agreements.[63]

Remember, just because you haven't formally created a team contract doesn't mean team norms don't already exist. Team members are already creating their own interpretations of "how we work," which can lead to confusion, silos, and frustration when collaborating. Build the contract together as a team, and you'll transform the culture you *think* you have into a culture you can *see and feel*, one defined by shared focus, clarity, and intentional action.

In the next section, we'll explore how to sustain and evolve your contract over time.

## Sustaining the Agreement: How to Keep the Contract Alive

Creating a team contract is one thing, but living by it is another. If it's not revisited, discussed, and reinforced, it will fade into the background like so many unused mission statements and wall posters. In this section, we'll explore how leaders and teams can ensure the contract stays visible, dynamic, and effective over time.

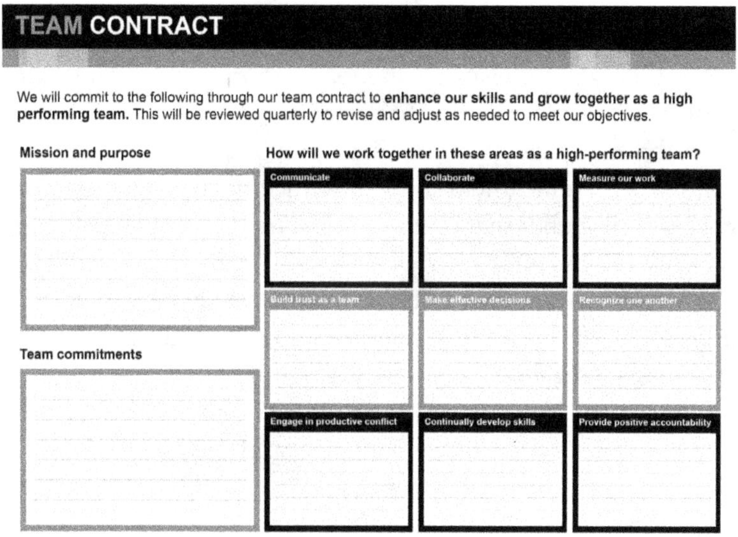

**TEAM CONTRACT**

We will commit to the following through our team contract to **enhance our skills and grow together as a high performing team.** This will be reviewed quarterly to revise and adjust as needed to meet our objectives.

**Mission and purpose**

**How will we work together in these areas as a high-performing team?**

| Communicate | Collaborate | Measure our work |
| --- | --- | --- |
| Build trust as a team | Make effective decisions | Recognize one another |
| Engage in productive conflict | Continually develop skills | Provide positive accountability |

**Team commitments**

Figure 10.3: The Team Contract

## Repetition Builds Reputation

People remember what gets repeated. Leaders who integrate the language of the contract into meetings, feedback loops, and celebrations build a shared vocabulary. Phrases like "let's circle back to what we agreed on in the contract" or "this aligns with our commitment to clear communication" reinforce the behavioral standards. The repetition doesn't have to be rigid; it just has to be intentional. Make the team contract part of your onboarding for new members, performance reviews, and goal-setting. Teams that do this report significantly higher engagement and cohesion over time.[64]

## Visual Cues and Accessibility

Keep the contract visible. One team printed theirs on a large poster and displayed it in their meeting space. Another added it to the first page of every client proposal deck, not to show off, but to remind themselves how they operate. A tech team created a Slack bot that posted one contract principle each week to spark discussion.

Visual reminders, coupled with storytelling, make the agreement stick. Leaders can share stories at team meetings, such as "Here's how I saw us living our contract this week," inviting team members to do the same. Tom and I have both witnessed the rise in engagement and enthusiasm as we sit in meetings with the teams we coach, who are now having meaningful discussions. They celebrate their differences and hold themselves accountable to a standard that has now been set. Remember, it wasn't dictated. The team created these behaviors, commitments, and norms together so they could understand what they could do to reach their full potential as a collective, not as individuals.

## Quarterly Reviews and Contract "Health Checks"

A contract is not set in stone. Teams evolve. Contexts shift. The best teams run quarterly "Health checks" to assess whether their norms are still working. Use simple pulse checks like:

- What parts of the contract are we living well?
- Where are we falling short?
- What needs to evolve based on how we've changed?

Hold consistent meetings together to discuss sections of the Team Contract during monthly meetings, quarterly off-sites, or at a minimum, biannually. Document the discussion and adjust the contract language accordingly. Re-signing the agreement can literally or symbolically reaffirm the commitments the team made to each other.

In addition, when you add new team members, make sure to review the process with them during onboarding. Ask them whether they feel something is missing. One team I coach has implemented this successfully, and on one occasion, the new team member pointed out that there is nothing about having fun together! It was an omission that the team later added successfully—with laughter, I might add, not knowing how they missed that initially.

## When Leadership Models the Agreement

The leader's role is pivotal. When leaders embody the behaviors outlined in the contract, the message is clear: this isn't performative. It's foundational. At a Boston-based marketing team, their managing partner openly reflected on where he fell short, stating, "I interrupted too often this week, and I'm working on it." After that, trust surged. Team members began offering similar reflections, not as a performance, but as a commitment to self-awareness and progress. They now felt as if permission had been given to admit these opportunities for improvement, and instead of being met with judgment, they were met with support.

This behavior of holding conversations together about public ownership of missteps links to Amy Edmondson's concept of "learning behavior" and its role in psychological safety.[65] It sends a message: Growth matters more than perfection. What a fantastic concept to celebrate, as we all know that failure is inevitable. We have all failed at some point, but did we feel safe asking for help, or did we feel we needed to hide our deficiencies for fear of retribution?

Remember, everyone on the team is a leader, and when we discussed the Collective Leadership Theory, it focuses on all team members setting the tone so that appreciation for each other's flaws can fuel continued learning and development as a team in the open, rather than individually in silence.

## Data-Driven Reminders

For more analytically inclined teams, integrate contract check-points into performance data. For example:

- Include a "collaboration" score in peer feedback forms.
- Use short surveys to assess psychological safety or alignment with norms.
- Ask clients for feedback on perceived team cohesion.

One software firm implemented a bi-weekly pulse survey with just two statements:

- I saw us live our team contract this week.
- I acted aligned with our contract this week.

Over six months, the consistency of positive responses correlated with improved sprint outcomes and higher Net Promoter Scores.

## Coaching Insight: Revisit with Curiosity, Not Criticism

When the contract drifts, and it will at some point, the tone of reconnection matters. A curious approach sounds like: "We noticed we've been slipping in responsiveness. What's changed? What would help us realign?"

That's different from a shaming tone: "We agreed to this—why aren't we doing it?" A team I worked with in financial services used their contract to reset after a tense quarter. Rather than blame, they started with a workshop titled, "What's still true about us?"That question anchored them in shared identity before moving to behavior.

## When the Contract Is Broken: Repairing Trust and Rebuilding Alignment

Even the most well-intentioned team contracts will be broken at some point. Not because people are careless, but because we are human. We get busy, we forget, we default to old habits. What distinguishes high-performing teams from the rest is not perfection; it is how they respond when the agreement is violated.

### Normalize the Drift

When a team member forgets to follow a contract behavior, say, responding to emails within 24 hours, it's easy for others to assume it's deliberate. However, most often, it's an unintentional drift. Normalizing this possibility creates space for dialogue. One team I worked with added this statement to their contract: "When we drift, we reset without blame." It gave them language to initiate repair. Instead of finger-pointing, team members could say, "Hey, I think we might be drifting. What steps can we take so that we can realign as a team?"

According to Kim Scott's framework in her book *Radical Candor*, teams benefit when they combine care with directness.[66] Addressing contract drift is one of those moments where candor, when tempered with empathy, can prevent lasting harm to team relationships.

### Repair Before You Rewrite

When breakdowns happen, the impulse is often to rewrite the contract, but first, the team must repair trust. A marketing team at a mid-sized asset management firm ignored their contract's conflict resolution clause for several months. Tensions mounted. People avoided difficult conversations, and workarounds replaced direct dialogue. Instead of rewriting the contract, they held a "truth-telling session" where each team member answered two questions:

1. Where have I fallen short of our agreement?
2. What do I need from this team to re-engage?

The exercise was uncomfortable but healing. The team didn't change the contract, nor did they need to. They needed to recommit to it this time with full awareness of what it meant.

## Revisit the "Why"

Repeatedly broken contracts may signal a deeper issue. Perhaps the norms were too aspirational. Or maybe the team never truly bought in. Re-centering the team on *why* the agreement exists helps reset the foundation.

Start with these coaching prompts:

- What's the cost of not living by this agreement?
- What would be possible if we did?
- What needs to be redefined—not just behavior, but belief?

Leaders play a critical role in modeling how to respond to broken agreements. When a leader says, "I didn't follow through on our agreement, and I'm sorry," it sends a powerful message. It makes accountability safe, not punitive.

In one law firm, a partner violated their agreement by canceling multiple weekly check-ins without notice. The team began to disengage. Rather than justifying his actions, the partner invited the team to help revise the check-in format so it worked for everyone. The message was: "I broke trust. Let's rebuild it together." This is another example of how, when things go wrong, which they will at some point, being able to have open discussions where any team member can show vulnerability and ask for support can strengthen the dynamics moving forward.

## Conclusion: Culture by Design, Not Default

When a team defines how they work together explicitly, collaboratively, and with care, they move from being a group of talented individuals to a collective force. A team contract is not about control; it's about co-creation. It makes the invisible visible and the assumed articulated. It builds bridges where silos tend to grow.

By exploring the values that matter most, the behaviors that bring those values to life, and the consequences of drifting away from them, teams create cultures of clarity, respect, and resilience. And when those agreements are reviewed, refined, and regularly recommitted to, the result is not only better performance but stronger trust. More than ever, organizations are realizing that performance metrics alone don't build high-functioning teams. Norms do. Agreements do. The quality of how people treat each other does.

This chapter laid out a framework to build that foundation. One that is adaptable to your team's unique dynamics and powerful in any industry. Whether your team is just forming or evolving into its next chapter, your contract is both compass and anchor because great teams don't happen by chance. They happen by choice, and this kind of intentional, collective choice is the heartbeat of every high-performing culture.

## Taking Action

1. Prepare your team for a discussion focused on creating the Team Contract.

   - What do we need to do to ensure everyone feels safe to share their thoughts and ideas?
   - How will we show up and be curious about what our team members want to share?
   - What can we do to prepare ourselves to have a growth mindset rather than a fixed mindset when making these commitments?

2. Choose three areas to focus on in each session instead of attempting to create each area at once.

   - Prioritize the areas.
   - Ensure there are no more than three or four commitments in each area to avoid overwhelming.
   - Make sure that commitments are actionable or measurable.

3. Once it is complete, discuss how often you will review it together as a team.

   - In what areas does the team feel they are performing well together?
   - What one or two areas can be improved upon? What steps will you take together as a team?

# CHAPTER 11

## Igniting Potential: Building a Culture of Coaching

*Be curious, not judgmental.*
—Falsely attributed to Walt Whitman
by Ted Lasso and others

## Moving from Management to Coaching: A Cultural Shift

In many modern organizations, leadership is evolving from a model rooted in hierarchy and control toward one centered on growth, trust, and empowerment. At the heart of this evolution lies coaching, not as an add-on practice for underperformers or executives, but as a foundational leadership capability. This chapter explores how building a culture of coaching unlocks team potential, drives engagement, and accelerates performance.

### Why Coaching Matters More than Ever

The traditional model of leadership emphasized directing, evaluating, and correcting. While those skills still have their place, they are insufficient in today's dynamic, knowledge-based environments where adaptability, creativity, and collaboration are paramount. Teams no longer respond well to leaders who tell them what to do—they thrive under leaders who help them uncover how to grow.

A coaching culture shifts the dynamic from hierarchy to partnership. According to the International Coaching Federation (ICF), organizations with strong coaching cultures experience 46 percent higher engagement, 42 percent higher productivity, and 38 percent higher customer satisfaction compared to peers without one.[67] Coaching isn't just a nice-to-have; it's a proven accelerator of team health and business success.

## Coaching as a Leadership Mindset

Coaching is fundamentally different from managing. Managing is about performance, and coaching is about potential. It prioritizes curiosity over certainty, listening over instructing, and ownership over compliance.

Consider a typical scenario in a leadership team. An emerging leader brings an issue to their manager. In a traditional model, the manager would solve the problem. In a coaching model, the leader might say: "What's your perspective on how to move forward?" or "What options have you already considered?" These simple questions elevate confidence and critical thinking—two attributes essential to long-term growth.

This mindset shift also impacts the broader team environment. In coaching cultures, feedback flows in all directions. Leaders model vulnerability by asking for feedback, and teammates are encouraged to reflect, experiment, and take risks.

## From Manager to Coach: The Three-Stage Journey

Becoming a coaching leader doesn't happen overnight. It unfolds in stages:

- **Awareness:** The leader recognizes the difference between directing and coaching. They understand coaching is a skill and commit to learning it.
- **Application:** The leader begins to integrate coaching questions and techniques into everyday conversations—especially during one-on-ones, team meetings, and performance check-ins.
- **Integration:** Coaching becomes a natural leadership style. The leader fosters a safe, empowering environment where others grow into their own leadership potential.

Each stage requires intention. Many leaders stall between Awareness and Application because they fear losing control. But the paradox of coaching is that by relinquishing control, leaders gain influence.

## Coaching Culture Continuum

A helpful way to visualize this shift is with a "Coaching Culture Continuum," which maps the stages from compliance-based leadership to coaching-based leadership.

| Stage | Culture Description | Leader Behavior |
|-------|---------------------|-----------------|
| **Compliance Culture** | Rules are followed; initiative is minimal | Directs, monitors, and corrects |
| **Performance Culture** | Goals are achieved; KPIs matter most | Motivates, evaluates, and rewards |
| **Development Culture** | Learning and growth are encouraged | Offers feedback and provides stretch opportunities |
| **Coaching Culture** | Trust, reflection, and shared ownership define team interactions | Asks powerful questions and empowers team development |

This continuum provides both a diagnostic and a roadmap. Where does your team operate today? What conversations are needed to move toward a coaching culture?

## Coaching Story: The Turnaround at Vista Analytics

When the executive team at Vista Analytics, a mid-sized data services firm, committed to coaching, they didn't start with HR. They started with themselves. Each leader committed to attending a coaching class to build this skillset. Companies such as Microsoft, Amazon, Boeing, and other Fortune 500 organizations have incorporated this into their leaders' curricula as they grow. They are given the opportunity to learn coaching competencies so they can shift their mindset and develop their coaching abilities.

Each executive engaged a coach and began practicing weekly peer-coaching sessions. Within six months, they reported more candid conversations, reduced rework, and faster decision-making. The shift was contagious. Team leads noticed the new language in meetings. Phrases like "What might be another way to look at this?" and "What are you learning from that outcome?" replaced blame and defensiveness. Within a year, the company exceeded its strategic targets—despite a volatile market.

Their story illustrates a core truth: coaching isn't just a skill. It's a signal. When leaders coach, they show the team that growth matters more than perfection.

## Creating the Conditions for Coaching to Thrive

Creating a coaching culture doesn't happen by accident. It requires intentional design, leadership commitment, and the psychological conditions that allow coaching to take root. Leaders often want coaching outcomes—ownership, growth, and initiative—but forget the environment needed to produce them. You can't coach someone who feels unsafe, unheard, or undervalued.

Psychological safety, trust, role clarity, and time are foundational to a culture where coaching sticks. Remember that research from Google's Project Aristotle found that psychological safety was the number one factor that distinguished high-performing teams from others.[68] Without it, even the best coaching questions fall flat.

## Coaching Moment: The Missed Opportunity

I once worked with a team leader, Darren, who had read every coaching book on the market. He understood GROW, knew how to ask open-ended questions, and even used a coaching journal. But his team resisted. One associate, Maya, privately confided, "He asks good questions, but I don't trust him. Last time I was vulnerable, he used it against me during our performance review."

This wasn't a skill problem. It was a "**conditions**" problem. Until trust was restored, no coaching tactic would work. Although coaching is about development, it can't be developmental if it's also perceived as evaluative or unsafe.

To be an effective coach, this team leader needed to make a couple of quick changes. First, have a conversation with this team member and take the feedback to heart. This specific example was unintentional because, given the behavior, what he had been taught previously about coaching was more in line with delivering a performance evaluation or, better yet, a performance plan.

Use this example to be curious about your coaching skills. Are you showing up to sessions with team members as an authoritarian leader or as a curious coach? These are two completely different skill sets.

## The Four Conditions That Support Coaching

Based on team effectiveness research, workplace psychology, and coaching implementation data, we can distill the conditions for coaching cultures into four foundational areas:

| Condition | Description | Why It Matters |
|---|---|---|
| **Psychological Safety** | Team members feel safe to speak, fail, and challenge without fear of retribution | Trust is the bedrock of vulnerability, learning, and feedback |
| **Role Clarity** | Individuals understand their responsibilities and where they have discretion | Without clarity, coaching creates confusion rather than growth |
| **Time and Space** | Leaders and teams have dedicated time for coaching and not just task management | Coaching cannot flourish in reactive, overloaded environments |
| **Trust in Intent** | Team members believe coaching is meant for development, not control | Coaching requires goodwill; people won't grow with someone they don't trust |

## Visual: Coaching Conditions Framework

| Coaching Culture Enabler | What It Looks Like | Leader Action |
|---|---|---|
| **Psychological Safety** | Team members speak up without fear; mistakes are learning opportunities | Normalize failure, ask for feedback, model vulnerability |
| **Role Clarity** | Clear responsibilities, expectations, and accountability structures | Define decision rights and align roles to outcomes |
| **Time and Space** | Time is protected for one-on-ones, reflection, learning, and coaching dialogue | Schedule coaching rhythms and de-emphasize reactive firefighting |
| **Trust in Intent** | Team members know feedback is for growth, not punishment | Lead with care, reinforce intent, avoid weaponizing feedback |

## Coaching Story: Elevating at Edgewater Financial

Edgewater Financial, a regional wealth advisory firm, struggled with employee turnover, especially among junior associates. The partners had initiated coaching training but saw little behavior change.

A leadership coach helped them take a different approach. Instead of starting with coaching scripts, they conducted a cultural audit using a "Coaching Readiness Index." The results revealed that only 32 percent of the team felt safe speaking honestly in meetings, and only 18 percent trusted leadership to have their back when mistakes occurred.

The partners were shocked. They thought they had a "tight-knit culture." The problem wasn't their intent; it was their assumptions. Over six months, the firm invested in rebuilding trust, creating role charters, and carving out coaching time in weekly agendas. Within the year, attrition dropped 40 percent, and client satisfaction scores rose for the first time in three years.

Edgewater didn't transform through technique. They transformed through **environment**.

## A Coaching Leader's Reflection Tool

To build coaching conditions, leaders must first **reflect on what they're signaling**. Here's a quick self-check:

- Do I allow space for dissent and disagreement?
- Have I clearly defined what each person owns and where they have autonomy?
- Have I scheduled coaching time—or just talked about it?
- Have I earned the trust to challenge someone toward their potential?

This reflection isn't just academic, it's strategic. Leaders who coach in high-trust, clear, and safe environments multiply impact. Those who coach in fear-based, chaotic cultures often unintentionally do more harm than good.

## Research Snapshot: Coaching in High-Trust Cultures

Research has long shown that when teams operate under high psychological safety—essentially, trust and freedom of expression—they exhibit more learning behaviors, greater information sharing, and better performance outcomes.[69] That kind of environment reduces the hidden cost of silence, fear, and disengagement, creating a foundation for sustained productivity and team cohesion.

In addition, multiple empirical studies demonstrate that supportive or transformational leadership—such as coaching, trust-building, and people-oriented behaviors—correlates with higher employee satisfaction, psychological safety, commitment, and performance. For example, a meta-analysis across 87 samples found strong effects on job satisfaction and performance under transformational leadership;[70] and a field study in commercial firms found that servant-leadership significantly predicted higher team performance and safety.[71]

## Are You a Whiteboard Coach?

I have lived two lives in my professional career: I was a senior leader in the financial services industry, and for the past decade, I've been an executive leadership and team coach. I started my leadership career as a branch manager, then as a regional manager, and later on a team of 400 with 12 direct reports.

Before my coaching sessions, I would "script the plays" on a whiteboard, like Bill Belichick, leading my team to win the big game. I would list the questions I planned to ask, the result I wanted to lead them to, and the tools I planned to give them to achieve it. Sometimes it led to victory, but it often led to burnout among team members because I expected them to do as I said without giving them the opportunity to share their own thoughts and ideas. Does this sound familiar?

When I shifted into becoming a leader who drove everything myself, I unintentionally left out the vision and voices of those who could have contributed essential ideas that might have elevated our success if everyone had felt fully free to bring their authenticity, engage deeply, and accelerate our performance together as a team.

Whiteboard coaching does not allow your team to reach its full potential. It overlooks the individual members' strengths, experiences, and diversity, which could lead to greater achievements and collaboration. I am honored and humbled to have a mentor, Janet Harvey, who taught me how to be a generative coach rather than a whiteboard coach. A generative coach will create space for your team members to create, innovate, and think through perceived obstacles, giving them a voice and contributing to their personal growth through their unique lens.

Meanwhile, a whiteboard coach outlines the steps to success based on their own experiences. This approach not only disengages members of your team but also prevents them from bringing their authentic selves to their roles and responsibilities. Instead of contributing their ideas, they nod along to whatever tasks they are given. Janet taught me that it is all about how we "view" our team members, guided by the following thoughts.

1. **See your team members as creative.** The individuals on your team have different strengths, and if you create space for them to be creative and use their ideas to develop new approaches, they will run with it and bring to life a process you would never have imagined.

2. **View your team members as capable.** Yes, I know it›s a shock, but they do not need you to give them step-by-step instructions on how to approach a situation. Give them support to find solutions themselves and trust they will be able to follow through. This will give them additional ownership and pride as a team member, as well as confidence in their unique abilities.

3. **Understand that they are resourceful.** Your team members are resourceful. Allow them to come up with solutions that can be part of the plays you script for them.

When you truly approach your coaching sessions in a generative way, you give your team members the gift of unlocking their full potential. You coach the wholeness of the individual in front of you and take away your need to draw up the plays. When your team members feel comfortable bringing their unique abilities to the table, the results are extraordinary and far more long-lasting because they stem from their exclusive thoughts and designs.

## Equipping Leaders to Coach Effectively

Most organizations say they want more coaching from their leaders, but very few equip those leaders with the confidence or capability to deliver it. Coaching is often seen as a "soft skill"—a nice-to-have rather than a core leadership function. But research shows that coaching conversations improve engagement, retention, and productivity.[72] If leaders are not trained and supported to coach, the culture cannot change.

### Coaching Story: From Directive to Developmental

At Orion Global Logistics, an operational VP named Rachel oversaw a team of 85 across four countries. Her managers hit metrics, but morale was plummeting. She described her style as "hands-on" and "results-driven," but employee engagement scores had declined for six straight quarters. HR encouraged her to explore coaching. At first, she resisted: "I don't have time to coddle."

Through an internal leadership development cohort, she was introduced to coaching techniques and practiced in peer groups. Over several months, Rachel shifted from giving answers to asking questions. Her first breakthrough came in a team meeting when she asked, "What am I not seeing here?" Silence broke. Then a team leader finally said, "We've been afraid to tell you—your feedback usually comes with punishment."

Rachel didn't defend herself. She just listened. That was the moment her team began to trust her again. One year later, her region had the **lowest turnover rate** in the company and the **highest innovation score** on the internal engagement survey. Rachel didn't change who she was. Instead, she expanded how she led.

## Coaching Competency Compass

To help leaders shift from managing to coaching, we introduce the **Coaching Competency Compass**—a practical guide to the four core dimensions of effective coaching leadership:

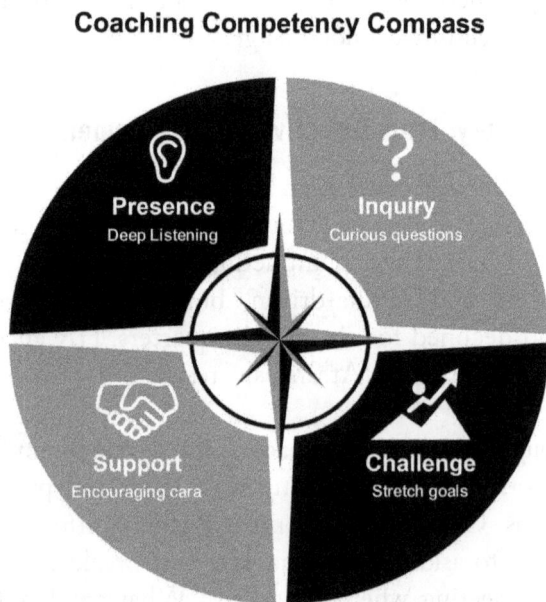

**Coaching Competency Compass**

Presence — Deep Listening
Inquiry — Curious questions
Support — Encouraging cara
Challenge — Stretch goals

**Figure 11.1: The Coaching Competency Compass**

| Coaching Dimension | What It Looks Like in Practice | Leadership Mindset Shift |
|---|---|---|
| Presence | Giving full attention, listening without judgment | From multitasking to mindful attention |
| Inquiry | Asking open-ended, forward-focused questions | From telling to discovering |
| Challenge | Encouraging stretch goals and deeper reflection | From comfort to constructive discomfort |
| Support | Creating accountability through care and consistency | From micromanaging to partnering for growth |

These competencies mirror core International Coaching Federation domains and can be adapted to any leadership context.

## Practical Coaching Prompts by Competency

Leaders can start coaching immediately by mastering a few well-placed questions:

### Presence
"Before we jump in—how are you really doing this week?"
"What feels most important for us to focus on right now?"

### Inquiry
"What have you already tried?"
"What's one option you haven't considered yet?"

### Challenge
"If success were guaranteed, what would you attempt?"
"What might be holding you back?"

### Support

"How can I best support your growth here?"
"When would it be helpful for us to check in again?"

Simple, consistent use of these questions helps leaders integrate coaching into daily interactions without needing a formal title or certification.

## Toolbox: The Coaching Micro-Moment

Not all coaching has to happen in a 60-minute one-on-one. Some of the most transformational coaching happens in **micro-moments,** which are brief, meaningful conversations inside meetings, hallway check-ins, or after-action reviews.

### Example

During a post-client debrief, a senior advisor asks her associate: *"What part of that meeting stretched you the most?"*

That one question shifts the tone from task execution to self-reflection and development. Research shows that embedding micro-moments of coaching into daily routines helps normalize feedback and learning across the team.[73]

## Barriers to Coaching Competence

Equipping leaders to coach is as much about **removing barriers** as it is about training skills. The most common barriers include:

**Time Pressure:** "I don't have time to coach."
*Reframe:* Coaching saves time over the long run by building independence.

**Fear of Overstepping:** "I'm not their therapist."

*Clarify:* Coaching is not therapy; it's about unlocking potential within the work context.

**Perfectionism:** "I'm not a certified coach."

*Empower:* You don't need certification to ask great questions and build trust.

**Culture of Control:** "If I don't give the answer, things fall apart."

*Challenge:* If that's true, it's time to rewire how the team solves problems.

Training alone won't overcome these. Leaders must **experience coaching themselves,** either as coachees or in peer-coaching environments, to build confidence.

## Coaching Moment: The First Coaching Conversation

During a team leadership workshop, a VP turned to his colleague and asked, "Can I try a coaching opener on you?" He leaned in and said, "If we had 15 minutes to work on something that would help you lead better this month, what would it be?"

The colleague blinked. "No one's ever asked me that."

The room fell quiet.

In that moment, this peer-to-peer interaction shifted the dynamics of the whole workshop. People weren't just hearing about coaching. They were doing it. This is an important behavior to model within your team's culture. Supporting each other's success, providing valuable feedback, and challenging others to reach their potential can be missing in some organizations.

Find time as a team to discuss how you could coach each other consistently. What would each individual need to feel comfortable? What would be the expectations for how to prepare? How will team members follow up with each other after these interactions?

### Research Snapshot: Why Coaching Competence Matters

In a study of 3,200 managers by the Center for Creative Leadership, leaders who practiced coaching behaviors had **20 percent higher team productivity** and **30 percent higher retention rates** compared to those who didn't.[74] The same study found that leader-driven coaching correlated strongly with psychological safety and innovation.

Another meta-analysis by Theodosiou and Papaioannou showed that leaders who coach with presence and inquiry **significantly increase employee goal clarity and intrinsic motivation**.[75]

## Sustaining a Coaching Culture Over Time

It's one thing to start a coaching initiative. It's another to **sustain a coaching culture**. The former requires skill and effort. The latter demands systems, consistency, and leadership courage.

Many organizations launch coaching with enthusiasm, implementing training sessions, coaching cards, and keynote speakers, but six months later, the energy fades. Why? Because coaching didn't become part of the operating system. It remained a "program," not a **way of working**. To build a coaching culture that lasts, leaders must embed it in how people think, meet, decide, and grow.

When I first started in a coaching role about a decade ago, it was a difficult transition because there were so many different definitions and experiences among leaders. And not many of them resulted in positive experiences. When I worked as a coach at Wells Fargo Advisors, my energy was high, my enthusiasm was through the roof, and whenever I was assigned a new leader, I treated it like a sport. I was revved up and ready to do everything in my power to reach the finish line of helping them establish the new skills that would undoubtedly help them thrive in their place of business.

However, not every leader shared my perception of coaching. Craig was one of those leaders. The first sentence Craig uttered to me was, "Bryan, just tell me what I did wrong so that I don't have to talk to you." Ouch, right? After I recovered from the comment, I realized that Craig's perception was the direct result of his past experiences.

Before our Field Leadership department was established, a leader could be assigned a coach from outside the organization. This was mostly an option if that leader had a performance issue that needed to be "fixed." This was common at the time, and unfortunately, we still have a way to go before coaching is fully viewed without the stigma of needing to "fix" someone.

Coaching is an option for an employee who wants to grow, develop, and build the skillset needed to reach both their personal and professional goals. The gap lies between the old way of thinking and the new, and I believe it can be fixed with a simple process. If Craig and I had met beforehand to set expectations for how we would both show up for the sessions and which discussion topics would be a priority, it might have gone differently. However, to no fault of Craig, his past coaching experience was showcased to him as a session designed to "fix him."

This is where there is a gap and a red flag that still waves around in companies today. A coaching culture needs to be established so much so that it becomes the DNA of every team, and every employee is well-versed in what coaching is. The process is viewed as far more than a "catch-up" conversation between coach and employee.

The steps below are designed to create intentionality in coaching, implemented to foster ownership and execution among team members.

1. **Hold a Contracting Conversation.** During this discussion, set the expectations for how each one of you, the leader and team member, will show up to these coaching conversations. Remember, as the coach, you want to view the employee as creative, capable, and resourceful. Be sure to communicate that you believe this about them in this first meeting.

   - **Set expectations by clarifying** what everyone's role is (coach vs. client) to prepare in advance for these sessions.
   - **Create accountability** so you can support each other during and in-between meetings.
   - **Enforce a cancellation policy.** I suggest notifying the other party at least 48 hours in advance if either party needs to move the coaching session.
   - **Accept responsibility.** At the end of the meeting, each party should accept their goals and provide specific action steps, a timeline, and information on how the team member can reach out for support between coaching sessions.

2. **Utilize the Coaching Update Form.** This is a tool I developed during my journey as a coach, designed to help leaders and teams be more productive. It can create a dynamic shift in your team members' mindset when they think about their coaching sessions. In most cases, leaders take on the responsibility of setting the agenda, walking through the topics, and checking in to see how they are performing. Instead, this places accountability

back on the team member so that accountability drives these coaching sessions. As a leader, you can now show up as a true coach, being present, reflecting, and discussing success and obstacles from the team member's perspective.

- Ask the team member to complete the one-page fillable PDF and send it back to you, the coach, at least 24 hours before the discussion.
- The form includes questions regarding their goals and priorities within a given time frame.
- It also asks them to reflect on their last coaching session and share what they accomplished. What didn't they accomplish? What got in the way?

3. **Follow Up and Follow Through.** This is where engagement and results can get missed in creating a coaching culture. Ensure that you instill a framework for reporting back on how they are seeing success in the areas identified during your coaching sessions, or, if obstacles arise, how they can be specific in identifying what they are so that you can support them in being successful.

All too often, as I mentioned previously, what is called "coaching" in the organization can be time to just catch up or even have negative emotions attached, such as anxiety and nervousness, because they are only critical feedback sessions. Everyone has a different experience and relationship with feedback, so discuss this openly so that, once again, expectations are established, with your focus on the present and the future. To be successful, we need to identify what is specifically occurring so it can be prioritized and, if appropriate, worked on to achieve the success envisioned by all members of the team.

## Framework: Sustaining Coaching Cultures

To keep coaching alive beyond the launch, four strategic levers are essential.

| Lever | Description | Example Practice |
|-------|-------------|------------------|
| *Ritualization* | Make coaching part of meetings, feedback, and conversations | "Start-Stop-Continue" round in team meetings |
| *Measurement & Feedback* | Track coaching behaviors and outcomes through surveys and feedback loops | Quarterly pulse check on perceived coaching culture |
| *Modeling by Leaders* | Senior leaders must walk the talk and be coached themselves | CEO participates in live coaching during all-hands sessions |
| *Peer Learning Networks* | Peer coaching and learning groups reinforce practice beyond formal training | Cross-functional coaching triads for goal setting and support |

## Sustaining the Mindset: Coaching Is Ongoing

Perhaps the most important element of a sustainable coaching culture is mindset. Coaching isn't a switch you flip; it's a **practice**. It requires:

- Repetition
- Curiosity
- Feedback
- Self-Compassion

It's okay for coaching conversations to feel awkward at first. That's part of growth. What matters is consistency, not perfection. And when leaders normalize **imperfection in coaching**, they build even more trust. Saying "I'm working on this" is often more powerful than pretending to be a natural coach.

## Leader Reflection Tool: Embedding Coaching

To stay intentional, leaders can reflect on these five questions each quarter:

1. Where am I embedding coaching into our team rhythms?
2. When was the last time I was coached by someone on my team?
3. What story did I share this month that modeled learning or growth?
4. What feedback have I requested—not just given—in the past 30 days?
5. Where am I holding space for development, not just delivery?

Leaders who regularly ask these questions become the culture carriers that coaching requires.

## Three Ways to Take Ownership of Your Coaching Sessions

As a team member, the way you approach your coaching sessions can determine the value you get from them. You can either use this time proactively to develop in areas important to you and your role, or it shows up on your calendar as a task you dread. Below are ways to shift your thinking in your coaching sessions so you take ownership and use this time consistently to grow professionally and personally.

1. **Be proactive.** When thinking about your coaching sessions, are they mostly agenda items that either your leader or coach comes up with for you to work on, or do you actively contribute to the agenda? It is your development, so how do you think about this time with your coach? Take a moment to block time on your calendar with purpose; specifically, think about topics that are important to you and that you want to focus on in your upcoming coaching sessions.

   Engage your coach to discuss the topics before you meet, so there is clarity on what you want to cover during your session. This way, it gives you a roadmap for success from your perspective and lets you make it your time rather than spending it reacting to what your coach suggests, thus making it their agenda.

2. **Create a road map of success.** How are you connecting your coaching sessions throughout the year? Do you focus on success measures and action items in your development? Are they aligned with the outcomes the organization is striving to achieve?

   All too often, I have witnessed both individuals and teams I have coached lack clarity about what they want to achieve in our sessions, which can eventually lead to a lack of value. There needs to be a foundational game plan, which I refer to as the "Road Map of Success." If I give you a clean whiteboard on which to write what you want to accomplish this year, what would that look like? What steps would you like to take so we can celebrate your success both professionally and personally? How will you or the team be held accountable when things are not on track so that you can flex in a different direction?

Having this clear vision is essential to tying your coaching sessions to activities worth your time and attention, so you can measure your progress and increase the intentionality of the time you commit to your coaching sessions.

3.  **Communicate progress consistently.** How many times have you been asked to create goals in January, held a discussion around them for a month or so, and then not revisit them until November or December in order to prepare for a year-end review? Sound familiar? If you can implement time to follow up on your goals and action steps throughout the year, how would that support your overall success?

    Take time to update your coach on your progress toward the commitments agreed upon at your last meeting before your next session. I ask the leaders I coach to send me at least 24 hours in advance what they have and haven't accomplished, any obstacles, and what is important to them to discuss when we get together.

    This allows those I coach to have structure in our sessions and to keep the focus on what is important to them and on accountability to their commitments. Now their development remains at the forefront throughout the year. Otherwise, you're in the gap between the clarity of creating new goals in January and the anxiety in December of "*what did I even accomplish?*" in preparation for the year-end meeting.

A coach should challenge you on topics important to your development and align with overall success measures. Your responsibility is to take ownership of what is important and what is missing and to be clear about what you want to accomplish. Implement the steps outlined above with your leader or coach and focus on taking ownership of this time. You will feel the value of this dedicated time and see results from your coaching sessions in the future. Do not allow this to be reactive or inconsistent, as you owe it to your team and stakeholders to show up as the best version of yourself.

## Conclusion: The Coaching Culture Multiplier

When coaching becomes the operating system of a team or organization, it doesn't just improve conversations; it changes the way people think, work, and grow. Coaching unlocks a deeper human capacity: the ability to see people not just as employees, but as creative, capable, and resourceful contributors.

Across this chapter, we've explored how coaching begins with mindset, is sustained through habit, and is multiplied through systems. It starts in one relationship, one conversation, one moment of presence. Then it grows. Coaching cultures are not built by a few skilled individuals; they are co-created by communities of people committed to learning, challenge, and care. When leaders model curiosity, when teams adopt feedback loops, and when organizations embed rituals and reflection into their routines, coaching becomes contagious.

Ultimately, a coaching culture is a trust culture. It's a space where people feel safe enough to stretch and supported enough to succeed. The organizations that thrive in the years ahead won't be those with the most policies or perks—they'll be the ones that build coaching into the very fabric of how they work together.

Let this chapter serve not as a conclusion, but as an invitation:

- To slow down and listen differently.
- To lead through inquiry, not just answers.
- To invest in others, not as problems to solve, but as potential to ignite.

Because when leaders coach, cultures shift. And when cultures shift, people rise.

## Taking Action

1. What steps do I need to take to see my team members grow in the following areas? Be specific.

   - Creative
   - Capable
   - Resourceful

2. How can I establish expectations with my team members so they show up ready and prepared for coaching sessions?

3. Where does the team need to spend time to elevate my coaching skills?

4. What commitments do I need to make, as well as ask of my team members, to create a consistent coaching culture?

# CHAPTER 12

# The Bullseye Approach

*A good coach can change a game.*
*A great coach can change a life.*
—John Wooden

## Tom's Aha Coaching Moment

Perched on a high-top chair at my kitchen island, I hung up the phone with mixed feelings. I had just concluded a two-hour development planning call with a VP of operations for an energy company based in Houston. Two weeks earlier, I had met him face-to-face, in his office, to conduct a five-hour executive assessment. He was driven, emotionally intelligent, and strategically minded. He had a lot to offer his organization, and he was a dream to coach. His goals were to do more, do better, improve himself and the organization around him, and best of all, he was eager to learn and open to my insights and suggestions.

As a business psychologist with the Leadership Practice at Deloitte, I have done hundreds of assessments with senior leaders. We typically offered a one-hour debrief with each executive assessment. This particular project involved a longer, two-hour session to allow each leader to build a detailed development plan. As I said, he was a coach's dream, and the two hours flew by. We had a rich conversation. I was able to build on his ideas, and he was able to build on mine.

However, there was something missing. While the VP on the other end of the line was having this conversation for the first time, this was not my first rodeo, and our talk seemed to be headed toward the same outcome I had seen repeatedly.

Here is how it started. We came across a developmental comment in his report about innovation. He completely agreed with my suggestion that this was an area of opportunity for him. In fact, he thought innovation was lacking across his team. What should he do about it? After a brief discussion, we both decided that hosting an innovation fair in his department was a great way to make progress in this area. We discussed what this could look like, and he was optimistic and motivated, ready to take the idea forward and make it happen.

Why wasn't I equally optimistic? Why was a creeping sense of regret and dissatisfaction tugging down my enthusiasm for this great idea? Like hundreds of development conversations before, this one was starting to feel like a story with an opening scene that grabs you, but never reaches a satisfying conclusion. In other words, what would happen when we were done talking and making notes in a development plan template? What would be the outcome of that development plan? Would the leader follow it? Would the innovation fair happen? Would it produce any ideas that the team applied to their work? Would they produce any meaningful results? Or would the development plan sit in a folder somewhere three clicks deep in some file on his PC's desktop?

My frustration came from a sneaking suspicion that the development plan was an exercise in its own right, and not just for this VP of Operations, but for many leaders and teams I had worked with throughout my career.

My guess is that you, the reader, have completed at least one development plan in your career, and at least one of those development plans lived up to my fear. I have a hunch that someone out there has completed multiple development plans that never saw the light of day. They're still sitting in a folder on your desktop, perhaps next to PDFs of old articles from Harvard Business Review or Fast Company that you always meant to read.

## Why Traditional Development Plans Fall Short

In theory, professional development plans are designed to inspire growth, reinforce accountability, and sharpen capabilities. In practice, they often fall flat. They gather dust in performance review portals, framed in abstract language that's disconnected from the daily rhythms of work. These plans tend to reflect a moment in time rather than an ongoing learning process. Static and generic, they quickly become irrelevant in dynamic team environments.

The deeper issue lies not in the intention, but in the design. Research on adult development suggests that many well-intended change efforts fail because hidden assumptions and competing commitments quietly work against behavior change, even when motivation is high (Kegan & Lahey, 2009). Traditional development plans rely on predictive assumptions: that we can know today exactly which skill sets we'll need six or twelve months from now, that learning follows a linear progression, and that intentions translate seamlessly into action. But modern teams face complexity, shifting priorities, and fast feedback loops. They need developmental models that are flexible, responsive, and tailored to their evolving context.

The story described above is not an isolated story. Research from McKinsey & Company notes that 70 percent of leadership development efforts fail to yield measurable behavior change.[76] A major reason? Organizations treat development as an event rather than a continuous cycle. Effective leadership growth requires feedback, experimentation, reflection, and micro-adjustments—not one-time declarations.

Furthermore, traditional plans often focus on competencies rather than capabilities. Competencies emphasize compliance or what a leader 'should' do. Capabilities, on the other hand, emphasize the adaptability of what a leader "can" do in real time, in messy, complex environments. To build those capabilities, teams need tools that meet them where they are, acknowledge the real challenges they face, and guide them in taking deliberate, incremental steps forward.

Bryan and I believe there is a new and better way to develop teams and their leaders, and the remainder of this chapter lays out a strategy called the Bullseye Method that enables you to pull together the ideas throughout the rest of this book to design a development plan that can make the most of your potential. We will get into the details in a minute, but at a high level, we believe team development plans that work do the following things:

- Anchor on real results for your organization
- Provide an agile and adaptive strategy that fits the dynamic environment where you actually work
- Unlock creativity and engagement by focusing on iterative experimentation rather than rote execution of a plan you drafted weeks or months ago

## Introducing the Bullseye Method

The Bullseye Method is a simple yet transformative framework for accelerating development and behavior change inside teams. It adapts agile thinking to the reality of team dynamics by prioritizing incremental growth, learning from real-world feedback, and creating a visual roadmap for accountability.

At its core, the Bullseye Method centers around a single question: "What would mastery look like for you in this area?" That becomes the "Mastery Goal," placed at the center of the bullseye. The next step is to build three concentric rings outward from that core, each representing a smaller, focused goal that moves the team or individual closer to mastery.

Some of you will recognize some principles of agile project management in the Bullseye Method. Incremental goals can be seen as sprints. The next goal is always driven by a debrief or retrospective about the last one. The plan is designed to adapt as circumstances change and new needs are uncovered through the process. Yes, this is on purpose. Yes, this is inspired by the impact agile methods have made on work in all kinds of ways over the past three or four decades. In fact, it is a wonder these ideas have not made their way to developmental planning. Is software development not a bad metaphor for developing a new team mindset? We think so, and we hope you will experiment with us as we try to drive new thinking into the team development space.

One more comment before we lay out the Bullseye Method. We want to acknowledge that many of you (most of you?) DO have an agile mindset about teaming, even if you DON'T have an agile methodology to match it yet. If you DO have an agile mindset, you have probably already done something different when your last development plan crumbled. Your plan bumped into a challenge, and you recognized the need to switch gears. You did it without anyone telling you. You probably improvised.

Bryan and I want that improvisation skill built into team development, front and center, in a rigorous way, rather than a saving grace for the handful of people wily enough to break the rules. You can drive team development in a way that is flexible, creative, and innovative, yet also rigorous and purposeful—in a manner driven by accountability for clear actions and achievements. If done correctly, you will set yourself and your team up to hit dead center in any target where you place your aim.

## Implementing the Bullseye Method

Unlike traditional development goals that are vague or overly ambitious, Bullseye goals are grounded in the team's current realities. They reflect what's happening on the ground—conflicts, challenges, experiments—and provide a structure for testing new behaviors, assessing impact, and refining direction. These layered goals help reduce overwhelm and support motivation by showing visible progress over time. The easiest way to learn it is to do it. So, let's start like this:

**Step 1:** Write down what you think your team needs to do better. For example, "We need to make quality decisions with greater speed."

**Step 2:** Write down a tangible goal, preferably quantitative, that your team would achieve if it were to do that thing you wrote down in Step 1. Following our example, "We should shave a week off our annual budgeting process if we make high-quality decisions with greater speed."

**Step 3:** Draw a bullseye with five concentric circles.

**Step 4:** In that middle circle, write "Mastery Goal" and then the thing you wrote in Step 2.

Now stop and look at what you have here.

**Bullseye Goal Framework**

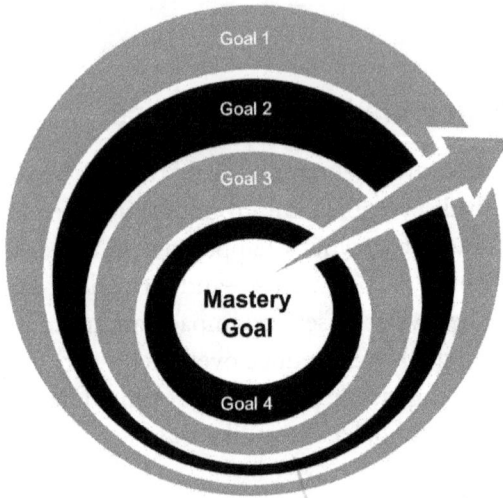

**Figure 12.1: Bullseye Goal Framework**

You are about to set four more goals that, if you were to achieve them, would put you in a great position to achieve goal five, the Mastery Goal. (Side bar: There is no magic to the number five, and once you get moving, you may even achieve the mastery goal in two or three goals. On the other hand, you may find you need to put in more work than expected, and you may need six or seven incremental goals to achieve your mastery goal.)

The idea is that these small, incremental goals will help you practice new mindsets and behaviors that drive the desired improvements in your team's performance. By keeping an eye on a big real-world goal that matters, you will avoid getting stuck in abstractions, and you will be able to ground your efforts in real-world contextual details that help you think about why your team struggles to make timely decisions with quality.

As progress is made, the outermost ring is filled in, signaling completion. Progress moves inward toward the core as a visual metaphor for closing the gap between current reality and desired mastery. This progression can be color-coded, discussed during one-on-ones, or even visualized on digital dashboards or physical posters. The image becomes a developmental "radar screen," making invisible effort visible to everyone. You may want to simply trust your gut when it comes to small goals that will help your team get there, but we will provide a fairly rigorous, structured approach to setting these four additional goals. This graphic reinforces a key insight: mastery is a journey, not a binary outcome. By celebrating each ring of progress, leaders help build momentum and morale.

## Example: Team Using the Bullseye Method

A mid-level product team in a SaaS company used the Bullseye Method to address internal friction and siloed communication. The team's Mastery Goal was "to operate as one team with shared priorities." Over a 10-week sprint, they progressed through three behavior experiments:

1. Hosting one rotating "shared stand-up" a week.
2. Building a transparent project board.
3. Aligning OKRs collaboratively.

By week 11, team members reported a 25 percent increase in perceived alignment (internal pulse survey), and the manager noted a reduction in the escalation of cross-functional issues. The Bullseye Method works best when integrated into existing cadences, such as weekly one-on-ones, retrospectives, and team meetings. It doesn't require new infrastructure; it just requires intentional design, visual accountability, and feedback loops that help teams connect behavior to purpose.

## SETTING INCREMENTAL GOALS

Begin with two questions designed to drive your thinking in two different directions:

1. Start with the problem in team dynamics: "Why don't we make high-quality decisions at speed, and what kinds of things might help us do this better?"

2. Start with the business problem reflected in the mastery goal: "Why do we barely hit our budgeting deadline every year, and what could we do to solve that?"

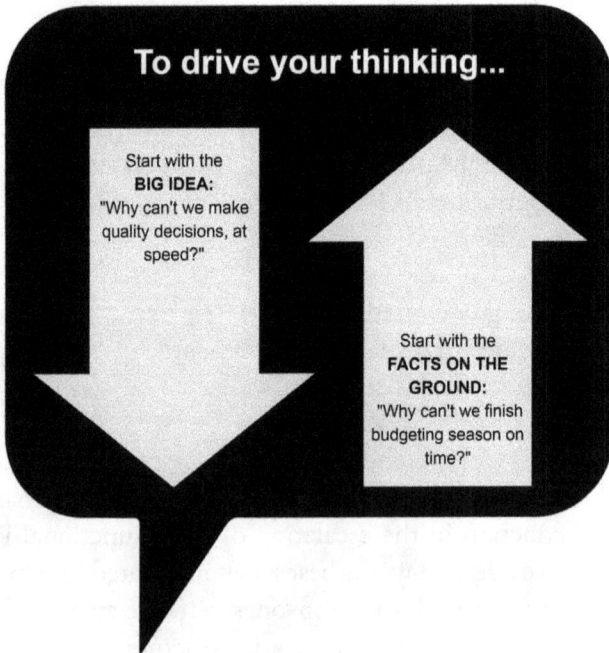

**To drive your thinking...**

Start with the **BIG IDEA:** "Why can't we make quality decisions, at speed?"

Start with the **FACTS ON THE GROUND:** "Why can't we finish budgeting season on time?"

**Figure 12.2: Thinking in Two Directions**

When you think in both directions at once, you avoid two common problems in team development.

**The first problem** is being too abstract and theoretical—essentially, too much focus on the first question. Reflection is an essential ingredient in team development, but where we have heard the most complaints from the teams we work with is that coaches do not do enough to push beyond reflection to direct application. This is especially true of senior teams that have engaged in extensive development work throughout their careers. Occasionally, an especially cynical leader has asked us, "Hey, this self-reflection feels great, but is it producing results, or is it just a rewarding exercise in its own right?" While we would counter that reflection is essential, and that there is nothing wrong with something being rewarding, we take this line of critique very seriously in our development work.

**The second problem** is when you become too concrete and literal—essentially, too focused on the second question. We all know a certain kind of teammate—often a results-oriented high performer—who looks at the question about the budgeting deadline and says, "Hey, if we want to be a week early in finalizing the budget, why don't we cut through the noise about these abstract notions of teamwork and just start a week earlier?" If that were the only problem, starting a week early would be a great solution. However, in most cases, the one challenging deadline is only a symptom of an underlying problem. No one would be asking the question if the only decision-making challenge showed up during the annual budgeting cycle.

We want the conversation about what will make your team better to be driven from both directions, as depicted below:

**Connecting Big Ideas to Facts on the Ground**

Big Ideas → Incremental Goals (Bullseye Rings) ← Facts on the Ground

Big Ideas
· Team Dynamics
· Mindsets
· Culture

Facts on the Ground
· Deadlines
· Constraints
· Real decisions

**Figure 12.3: Connecting Big Ideas to Facts on the Ground**

We want some big theoretical idea about what could make our team more effective to drive our thinking in one direction, and we want some facts on the ground to drive our thinking in another direction. This productive friction will drive us to identify four (or three or five) goals we can set to move everything in the right direction.

At this point, we encourage you to leverage any available data on your team (e.g., DISC), but the bullseye method recognizes that you may not have this data, and even if you do, it may only capture part of the story.

As a team, we need to develop some hunches about what the customer (in this case, the indecisive team) really needs. Let's fall back on the two driving questions ("big idea" and "facts on the ground") and use our imaginations to see what this might look like.

**A hunch about why the team is indecisive in general:** *"I think it's because we're afraid to be assertive or say anything controversial, so it takes a long time to get to the point."*

**A hunch about why the budgeting process is always a challenge:** *"The numbers-oriented members of our team have a hard time saying yes to budgeting items that are harder to nail down quantitatively (e.g., opportunistic spend on a brand-new marketing campaign)."*

Working from those two hunches, we will construct a "first draft" of goals one through four. The first few goals should focus on helping the team become more comfortable being assertive and handling "controversy." The last few goals should focus on the tension between quantitatively minded team members and those who are more intuitive and qualitative.

As we go, in true agile fashion, we are only going to pin down things we are confident will pin down. This is a recognition that each goal will be an experiment that could yield new information, causing us to pivot in a different direction. Just as we are watching a customer play with a prototype of a new smartphone, we do not know whether the three camera lenses on the back will strike the user as a cool new feature or a deal-breaker.

Keeping it simple, concrete, and high-level, we will set the goals:

1. Conduct one meeting with a very structured format that can force uncomfortable topics more into the open.
2. Conduct one meeting in which we discuss uncomfortable topics without a supporting structure.
3. Discuss one budgetary challenge, with an explicit focus on getting challenging topics out in the open.
4. Make decisions on that area of the budget before team-wide budget planning.

After thinking about both the "big idea" behind your challenges and the facts on the ground, set a series of incrementally more challenging goals where, if you achieved them, you are making progress on your team's biggest development opportunities.

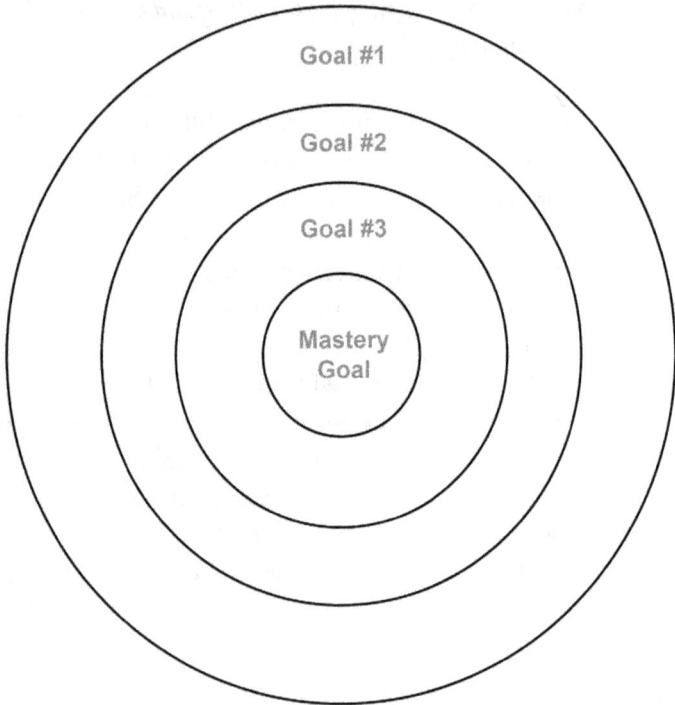

Goal #1

Goal #2

Goal #3

Mastery Goal

**Figure 12.4: Coaching with the Bullseye Approach**

This should all lead naturally to a faster decision-making process for the budget, achieving the Mastery Goal.

Notice that we have not filled in all the details for each goal. For example, we need a little information about how Goal #1 will proceed to set Goal #2. For now, we need to provide more detail on Goal #1. There could be any number of structured formats that could deliberately force uncomfortable topics out into the open, but our team will try the following.

## GOAL #1

- Lay out one decision and the options for moving forward.
- Pause the meeting for five minutes.
- Each member of the team writes down one thing they like and one thing they dislike for each option.
- The team re-engages in a roundtable sharing exercise: each member shares one positive and one negative about each option. For any repeats, they simply say "+1 to Andrea."

Let's say Goal #1 was a success. Teammates felt a newfound freedom to express disagreement openly and realized they could do so without offending one another. We recommend tracking progress visually. This serves as an "information radiator," another concept common to agile methodologies, designed to make information about progress toward a goal visible to the public. These drive both motivation and accountability.

Because it went so swimmingly, they decided that Goal #2 will be to simply ensure that one point of disagreement is brought out into the open on each decision discussed during their next meeting.

## GOAL #2

- During our next meeting, each decision will have at least one point of disagreement before moving on, and we don't overdeliberate any specific issue unless it is warranted.

Essentially, the team has taken the training wheels off and is engaging in comfortable, robust disagreement where necessary in a more organic way.

In some situations, this might uncover some other challenges that need to be addressed, but let's imagine it went well. From here, the team needs to achieve its goal of addressing one specific budgetary challenge. Let's imagine that, through the previous two goals, they realize that much of the challenge stems from differences in how finance and marketing view the ROI of various efforts. Rather than rushing to solve that, the next goal should focus on pushing further into that sensitive topic.

## GOAL #3

- Host a meeting where half the time is spent listening to marketing's priorities and their perspective on the smartest way to spend the marketing budget, then switch and let finance explain their priorities and perspectives.

Notice how low-pressure that goal was. This is where being incremental can be very important. While nothing transformational was accomplished in that one meeting, you can see how the obstacles that added time pressure to last year's budgeting cycle might start to look more manageable this year, and the team is more comfortable navigating disagreement.

Now, let's use our imaginations again and pretend finance has told marketing they would much prefer marketing to provide a precise estimate of the ROI of their spend. Marketing comes back and explains there is a new digital channel to market, and while they know they can reach more of the Total Addressable Market (TAM) if they take a risk and position their advertising on this new channel, there is no way to calculate exactly how many more customers will see it and buy the company's products.

The next goal is to make decisions about this budget area. The team is ready to add some more specifics to their draft version of this goal.

## GOAL #4

- Develop a framework for marketing spend and decide on next year's budget.
- Framework must acknowledge ROI.
- Finance must be involved at the front end to increase the rigor around estimates and prevent their concerns from emerging near the end of the budgeting cycle.

The team develops a marketing budget, with a finance partner joining the end-to-end process on the marketing side. Collectively, they make best-case, worst-case, and most-likely-case estimates, setting aside uncertainties, and they have a marketing budget decided upon before the rest of the budgeting occurs.

Now, let's think about what has likely happened to this team through this process. Based on what they were able to do, they likely have:

- A greater sense of psychological safety, with increased permission to disagree without fear of derailing team efforts or offending each other.
- A greater ability to take another teammate's perspective.
- New skills around developing quick, good-enough decision-making approaches that work for diverse areas of the team that face different sets of constraints.

Research on psychological safety shows that teams learn and adapt faster when members feel safe to speak up, challenge ideas, and experiment without fear of negative consequences.[77]

All of these should translate into faster decision-making during this budgeting cycle and generalize to other decisions the team needs to make. At this point, the team will have improved specific soft skills, such as being assertive and listening to teammates with diverse opinions, as well as hard skills, such as building frameworks to make decisions on complex, cross-functional challenges. Heading into the discussion of the entire budget, it should be easy to get through the process a week earlier than last year.

The team can fill in the innermost ring of their bullseye and celebrate their achievement.

At the outset, the goal seemed truly complex and inscrutable. However, they achieved a solution by following a few simple principles.

1. Experiment with a general hunch about what is holding the team back.
2. Identify specific activities in the flow of work that would elicit progress on this challenge.
3. Pay attention to what works and what doesn't at each step of the way.
4. Stay focused on the team's larger goal.

## Mastery and Momentum

Mastery is not a one-time destination; it's a mindset, a discipline, and a continuous journey of refinement. The Bullseye Method reframes mastery not as perfection, but as purposeful, evolving alignment between intention and action.

In many organizations, high-performing teams don't wait for permission to grow. They experiment constantly, they reflect often, and they refine relentlessly. What sets them apart is not talent alone; it's momentum. The Bullseye creates that momentum by translating big ideas into small, meaningful steps.

One of the most powerful practices we've seen is "the Mastery Goal reset," a quarterly ritual in which a team reviews its Bullseye progress, evaluates what has been learned, and sets a new Mastery Goal for the next 90 days. This creates a visible, aligned, and adaptive learning rhythm. Teams are no longer reacting to goals; they're evolving them.

Momentum also comes from public celebration of progress. In a regional credit union, teams began presenting their Bullseye progress in monthly all-staff meetings. One department focused on reducing onboarding confusion. Their Mastery Goal was "a seamless first 30 days." After completing each goal ring, like rewriting welcome packets or assigning onboarding buddies, they filled in their bullseye live on-screen.

Not only did this build energy and pride, but it also encouraged other departments to adopt similar developmental practices. This loop matters. Teams that revisit and iterate their Mastery Goals show stronger ownership, deeper collaboration, and higher psychological safety. The bullseye gives them a shared developmental identity, not just a set of tasks, but a narrative of becoming.

Finally, mastery is personal. As leaders introduce this method, they model its use for their own growth. Imagine starting a team meeting with: "Here's the bullseye I've been working on this quarter, and my goal was to lead more effectively in ambiguity. Let me show you what I've learned so far." That vulnerability sets the tone. It tells the team that development is not reserved for the struggling. Instead, it's the practice of the committed.

The Bullseye Method is a framework, yes. But more importantly, it's an invitation. To build, reflect, and evolve together. To move beyond checklists and into continuous capability building. To create momentum, not just for performance. It's aligning for growth that sticks. When teams own that rhythm, the bullseye isn't just a target. It becomes a mirror, a guide, and a shared map to becoming better together.

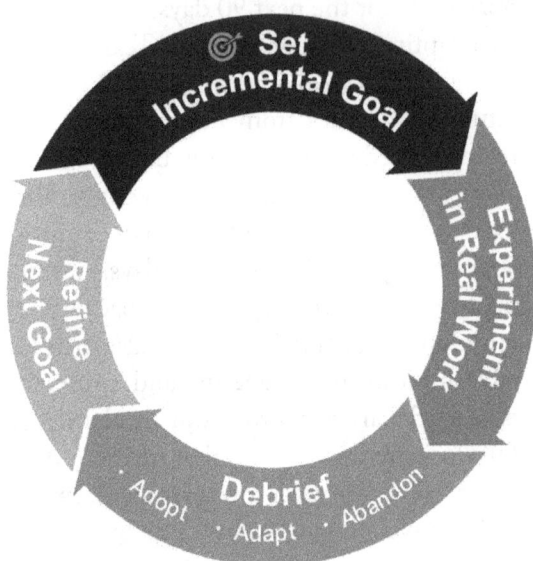

Figure 12.4: The Bullseye Learning Loop

## Conclusion: The Bullseye as a Culture Catalyst

At its core, the Bullseye Method is more than a framework for development; it's a catalyst for cultural change. It reframes growth as a shared, visible, and dynamic pursuit. It invites teams to move beyond vague aspirations and into concrete, behavior-focused progression.

By offering a visual map for incremental success, the Bullseye gives teams the confidence to act and the clarity to learn. It shifts development from being an HR-driven event to a leader-led rhythm. It doesn't demand perfection. Instead, it rewards intentionality.

Most importantly, the Bullseye Method strengthens a team's developmental fabric. It normalizes feedback. It honors progress. It sparks dialogue. And when used well, it ignites something deeper: a belief that mastery is not reserved for the exceptional but is accessible to all who are willing to reflect, adapt, and grow.

Let this method be more than a model. Let it be a mindset. A practice. A shared map for how your team becomes not just better at work but better together.

## Taking Action

After walking through that illustrative example, here are the end-to-end instructions one more time:

**Step 1:** Write down what you think your team needs to do better.

**Step 2:** Write down a tangible goal, preferably quantitative, that your team would achieve if it were to do that thing you wrote down in Step 1.

**Step 3:** Draw a bullseye with five concentric circles.

**Step 4:** In that middle circle, write "Mastery Goal" and then the thing you wrote in Step 2.

**Step 5:** Set four incremental goals that should set you up to achieve the Mastery Goal, using the following process:

- Start with a big question about team dynamics
- Ask an "in the weeds" question about a related problem on the ground

- Goal 1 should be more driven by the big question
- Goal 4 should be more driven by the contextual question

**Step 6:** For each goal, experiment with a new behavior or mindset to achieve it, then debrief using "Adopt, Adapt, Abandon."

## ADOPT, ADAPT, ABANDON

For teams that want a structured debrief after each goal, we recommend a simple approach familiar to anyone trained in Lean Manufacturing or Six Sigma Methodologies. Simply break down everything that happened and decide which pieces to adopt, adapt, or abandon:

- ADOPT anything that works
- ADAPT approaches that show promise but did not go perfectly
- ABANDON anything that does not work

**Bullseye Instructions:**

- Set a "Mastery Goal" - The goal should easily complete the sentence: *If I ever achieved_____, that would be a clear indication I had made progress on {development areas}.*
- Think backward and come up with some simple ideas about what incremental goals, activities, or achievements would be that you would have to move through to achieve that mastery goal.
- Translate those into clear, specific goals that are achievable but challenging.
- If you cannot think of a clear path including multiple goals leading to the Mastery Goal, that's fine; just come up with a first goal that is relevant, and once achieved, you can set the next goal.
- As you achieve each goal, fill in the color of the ring for that goal; this makes the bullseye an "information radiator;" it tracks your progress visually, enabling you to see your progress and how close you are to mastery.
- If you get stuck, fantastic! Explore what got you stuck and treat it as "data" about the subtle challenges you have in this area that could not be gotten to through a 90 minute assessment or a coaching conversation removed from your day-to-day.
- Independently or with a coach, mentor, manager, or friend, think about how to set a different version of that goal to gain traction and get back on track.
- The whole idea is that your development has to happen in the flow of work, and it is almost impossible to plan it out perfectly; however, you need some kind of structure to hold you accountable and make progress tangible.

# CHAPTER 13

## There Is No Finish Line

*Coming together is a beginning; keeping together is progress; working together is success.*
—Henry Ford

### The Journey Toward an Empowered Team

From the very beginning of this book, we've invited you to think about teams not just as groups of people working together, but as ecosystems capable of remarkable transformation. We've challenged the traditional paradigms of productivity, efficiency, and hierarchy by suggesting that the most effective teams live at the Efficient Frontier, defined by two powerful ingredients: authenticity and engagement. It's here, in the stretch zone between comfort and complexity, that transformational performance happens.

The Efficient Frontier is not a destination. It's a pursuit. Like its namesake in investing, it represents the optimal trade-off not between risk and return, but between vulnerability and commitment. Teams that get there don't stumble upon it. They design toward it. They choose to work in ways that amplify trust, align purpose, and elevate each member's potential.

Across this book, we've explored the practices and postures that help teams make this journey. We began with a foundational truth: "teams are stories in motion." Each team has a narrative that is shaped by culture, history, identity, and belief. Teams that shift from transactional to transformational don't just add better tools; they also shift their mindset. They rewrite the story they tell themselves and each other. They reclaim the narrative of what's possible.

In our own coaching work, we've seen this time and again. A team stuck in reactivity learns to listen deeper. A team siloed in functional roles begins to share accountability. A team wary of feedback starts practicing reflection. These small movements are anchored in intentionality, which starts to reshape the curve, and over time, the team begins to bend toward its frontier. This transformation doesn't happen by accident. It is nurtured through deliberate conversations, habits, and courageous choices. It is rooted in psychological safety, a concept defined by Amy Edmondson as a shared belief that the team is safe for interpersonal risk-taking.[78] Without it, teams regress to compliance. With it, they unlock creativity, dissent, and ownership.

The frontier also demands engagement, which is a sense of personal investment and energy that fuels performance. Gallup's research continues to affirm that highly engaged teams show 23 percent greater profitability, 18 percent more productivity, and 43 percent less turnover.[79] But engagement is not gifted; it's earned through purpose, clarity, and connection. To navigate toward the Efficient Frontier, teams must stop chasing only output and begin cultivating input. This includes shared purpose, inclusive dialogue, and a commitment to becoming together.

Teams that grow in this way redefine success not just as what they deliver, but how they show up, what they learn, and whom they become in the process.

## The Efficient Frontier Is a Journey, Not a Destination

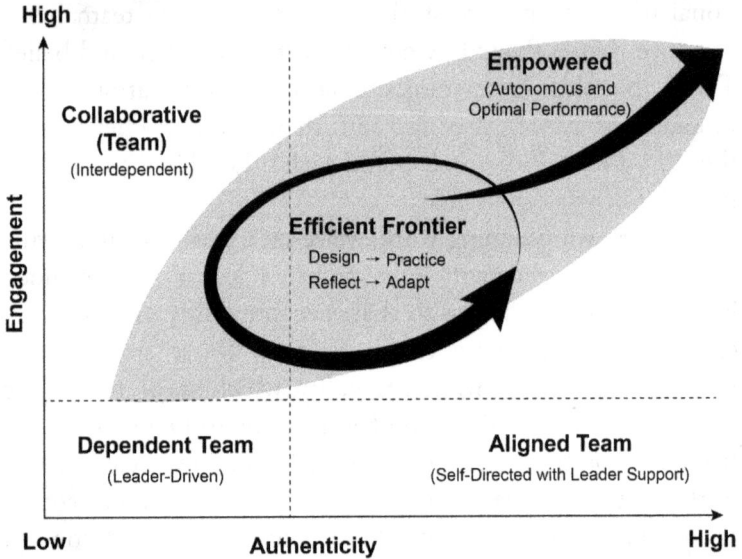

Figure 13.1: The Efficient Frontier of Teaming Revisited

Right now, you may be asking: where is my team on this curve? And perhaps more importantly: what story are we telling about who we are? Chapter 13 is not a ribbon-cutting; it is a mirror and a map. Because once you've glimpsed the frontier, you can no longer settle for the middle. The journey ahead is uncertain, but the path is clear: more courage, more clarity, more connection. This is where transformation begins, not at the finish line, but at the moment you choose to move forward, together.

## The Practice of Becoming: Adaptive Leadership in Action

To lead a team toward the Efficient Frontier requires more than systems or slogans. It demands a shift in posture. This is where adaptive leadership becomes not just relevant, but essential. As leaders, we are no longer the fixers, the solvers, or the sole stewards of vision. Instead, we become facilitators of potential, curators of clarity, and cultivators of momentum.

This model of leadership stands in contrast to the industrial era blueprint. The traditional leader was defined by control, expertise, and decisiveness. The adaptive leader is defined by humility, flexibility, and self-awareness. The former leads from the front; the latter leads from beside and behind. Research on leadership adaptability reinforces the shift, showing that leaders who consistently adjust their thinking, behavior, and decision-making in response to changing conditions are more effective at sustaining team performance and alignment over time.[80] In Chapter 6, we introduced a framework that both Tom and I have lived by for decades of coaching and executive leadership: the Collective Leadership Model, built around five catalytic behaviors: Curiosity, Collaboration, Appreciation, Adaptability, and Ownership.

These are not abstract ideals; they are daily practices, and within the teams that live them, something remarkable unfolds: friction becomes fuel, conflict becomes creative, and leaders turn from managers into multipliers.

Let's take each of these briefly:

## Table 13.1: The Collective Leadership Model

| Attribute | Description |
| --- | --- |
| **Curiosity** | The mindset of exploring ideas without judgment, inviting questions, and seeking to understand rather than assume. |
| **Collaboration** | The practice of co-creating solutions by combining perspectives, skills, and efforts toward a shared purpose. |
| **Appreciation** | The discipline of recognizing value in each person's contribution and expressing gratitude consistently. |
| **Adaptability** | The capacity to adjust approaches, roles, and expectations fluidly in response to changing circumstances. |
| **Ownership** | The commitment to personal accountability and collective responsibility for the team's outcomes. |

Together, these leadership behaviors align with the Center for Creative Leadership's definition of "boundary-spanning leadership," the ability to bridge divides to foster alignment, trust, and innovation.[81] In today's cross-functional, hybrid, and rapidly shifting environments, this style is not optional; it's critical. Adaptive leadership begins with self-leadership. As Goleman argued in his seminal work on emotional intelligence, the best leaders know how to regulate their own responses, interpret emotional data, and respond with intentionality.[82] This emotional fluency becomes the upstream force for building healthy teams.

The Practice of Becoming is, in its essence, a daily discipline of staying open. Open to feedback. Open to difference. Open to your own growth edges. It doesn't require you to have all the answers, but it does require you to remain committed to learning.

One of our clients, a rising leader at a biotech firm, reflected that her biggest leadership breakthrough came not through formal training but through a moment of silence. One in which she chose not to defend her position but to invite her team to question it. That moment, she said, was the beginning of shared leadership.

This is adaptive leadership. It is responsive, human-centered, and courageous. And it is the posture that invites teams not just to change what they do, but to change who they become together. As you read this, consider: Which of these practices are already part of your leadership DNA? Which needs strengthening? And who around you could help accelerate your own growth?

There is no finish line to leadership, not because we are never enough, but because becoming is a lifelong process, and the teams that thrive are those led by learners.

## Shared Language, Shared Identity: Sustaining Culture Through Rituals

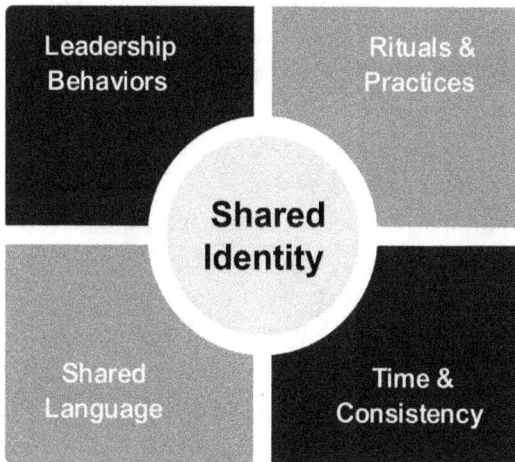

**Figure 13.2: Creating Shared Identity on a Team**

Culture doesn't happen by accident. It is shaped, reinforced, and sustained through intentional language and ritual. Throughout this book, we've underscored the idea that high-performing teams aren't just aligned in goals; they are aligned in meaning. They share language. They create symbols. They embed values in routines.

Rituals are the repeated behaviors that become meaningful for a team. These aren't limited to celebrations or retreats, as they include team huddles, goal check-ins, peer feedback loops, and even how we start and close meetings. According to Daniel Coyle, rituals create belonging and reduce uncertainty.[83] They send social signals about what matters and what is expected.

Take the example of a leadership team that began every Monday by revisiting their Team Contract, which for them is a simple five-minute touchpoint where members re-ground themselves in shared commitments such as "assume positive intent," "challenge with care," and "stay curious longer." That small ritual transformed the emotional tone of their meetings and shaped how they dealt with conflict.

Rituals also serve as cultural compasses. When deployed consistently, they cultivate habits of thought and behavior that reinforce psychological safety and trust. This was evident in our exploration of tools like the Team Contract and the Bullseye Method, which are not just frameworks but rhythmic practices that teams can revisit and evolve.

The Bullseye Method, in particular, provides a ritual for individual and team goal-setting, reflection, and experimentation. Rather than a static development plan, it becomes a living document. A roadmap that tracks both growth and mindset. Leaders who introduce the Bullseye ritual into monthly one-on-ones and team strategic meetings report deeper conversations and more authentic alignment.

Rituals also help sustain identity. Shared language becomes shorthand for shared purpose. In our coaching engagements, we've seen teams develop their own lexicons: phrases like "stay above the line," "progress over perfection," or "call it early" become part of the cultural DNA. These phrases encode behaviors and keep values top of mind. However, sustaining culture through rituals requires consistency and intentionality. It's not about volume, it's about resonance. Too many rituals dilute impact; too few create drift. As Ed Schein noted, the leader's primary job is to embed and transmit culture. Rituals are one of the most powerful tools to do that.[84]

One powerful example came from a healthcare team that added 10 minutes of "authentic wins" to every all-hands meeting. Team members would name something they saw in a colleague that aligned with their core values. Not only did this improve morale, but it also increased cross-department collaboration by 40 percent over six months. These rituals aren't fluff; rather, they are performance enablers. Research from MIT's Human Dynamics Lab found that the most successful teams had consistent communication rhythms and patterns that reinforced connection.[85]

As you look to the road ahead, ask yourself: What language defines our team? What rituals are shaping our identity? What culture are we reinforcing when we're not paying attention? When culture becomes intentional, it becomes exponential. And when shared identity is rooted in rituals, the team doesn't just survive change; it transcends it.

## Making the Choice to Lead Differently

The metaphor of "no finish line" isn't a signal of exhaustion, as it's a declaration of potential. Leadership is not a destination; it's a discipline, and the most effective leaders are not those who climb fastest, but those who keep moving forward, attuned, awake, and anchored to purpose.

Throughout this book, we've witnessed the journey from dependent to empowered teaming. We've introduced tools like the Efficient Frontier, the Collective Leadership Model, the Bullseye Method, and the Team Contract, but none of them matter if they remain mere theory. Leadership is not lived in concepts; it's lived in choices, and it is everyone's responsibility on a team to participate as leaders, regardless of their titles or roles.

- The choice to listen more than speak.
- The choice to build trust before driving performance.
- The choice to ask questions that don't have easy answers.
- The choice to believe that others are capable, resourceful, and creative.

These are the choices transformational leaders make daily—not perfectly, but intentionally.

When Tom and I first began to write this book, we weren't interested in repackaging tired frameworks. We noticed something missing in modern organizations: a respect for the human element of teaming. Not just process improvement or productivity hacks, but courage, connection, and creativity. This book is our response to that gap. Our method is both structured and flexible. It respects both the data and the story. It values clarity, but never at the expense of compassion. And it assumes that within every team lies untapped brilliance if only someone will ignite it.

## So, How Do You Lead Differently?

Start with reflection. Use the self-assessment tools provided in earlier chapters. Identify where you and your team land on the Efficient Frontier. Then choose one behavior that you want to develop over the next 30 days.

Build rhythm. Introduce a new ritual or revisit an old one. Bring the Bullseye Method to your next one-on-one. Create a Team Contract. Ask your team: What does trust look like here? Invite feedback. Not the anonymous, once-a-year kind— but real, relational, right-now feedback. And respond to it with curiosity instead of defensiveness.

Share what you're learning. Leadership isn't about having all the answers; it's about modeling the learning process. All team members need to feel empowered to contribute to the team's leadership in their own way. The culture needs to be one focused on empowerment and accountability. Here are a few things to get you curious about developing your skills in this area.

## Leadership Checklist: Choosing the Path Forward

- I've identified one behavior I want to strengthen.
- I've scheduled time to reflect weekly on my leadership growth.
- I've invited honest feedback from my team.
- I've facilitated at least one conversation using the Bullseye Method.
- I've articulated the "why" behind our team's work.
- I've acknowledged a teammate's contribution in the last seven days.
- I've asked someone, "What does support look like for you right now?"

These are not tasks to complete once. They are the rhythm of a new way of leading.

You don't have to lead perfectly, but you do have to lead on purpose.

# THE EFFICIENT FRONTIER OF TEAMING: COACHING PROMPTS

## 50+ Coaching Prompts

### 1. Building Trust and Psychological Safety

What helps you feel safe to speak your truth on this team?
When was the last time you felt truly heard here?
Where do you think silence might be masking uncertainty or disagreement?
What would it take for us to increase our trust score by 20 percent?
How do we respond when someone takes a risk, and it doesn't go as planned?

### 2. Clarifying Vision and Purpose

What part of our mission statement feels most personal to you?
If our team disappeared tomorrow, what gap would the organization feel?
What's the "why" behind your work?
How aligned are our day-to-day efforts with the outcomes we care about?
Where might we be chasing activity over impact?

## 3. Adaptive Leadership and Empowerment

What kind of leadership does this team need from me right now?
Where am I over-functioning and disempowering others?
Who has untapped potential we're not yet fully utilizing?
What decisions could the team make without me?
When was the last time I asked for feedback about my leadership?

## 4. Strengths, Style, and Self-Awareness

What's your superpower on this team?
What should we know about how you like to communicate?
How do your DISC traits show up under stress?
Where do your natural strengths become liabilities?
What's one blind spot we could help each other uncover?

## 5. Accountability and Clarity of Expectations

Where is accountability clear? Where is it murky?
How do we hold each other to a high standard—without blame?
What happens when a deadline is missed?
Who owns what on this project, and what does success look like?
What does healthy conflict look like on this team?

## 6. Feedback and Growth Conversations

What feedback have you been sitting on?
What kind of feedback do you find most valuable?
What's one thing I do that helps—or hinders—your success?
When do we debrief and reflect after big milestones?
How safe is it to offer upward feedback here?

## 7. Team Contracting and Working Agreements

What behaviors will make or break this team?
What do we each need to feel effective and included?
How will we respond when our working agreement is violated?
How do we decide when to meet, email, or use Slack?
What does responsiveness mean to us?

## 8. Measurement and Results

What does "great" look like for this initiative?
What leading indicators should we pay attention to?
Are we measuring what matters—or what's easy?
How do we track team health, not just performance?
Where could we use a visible scoreboard?

## 9. Team Identity and Culture

What's our team known for—and is it what we want to be known for?
What behaviors do we celebrate?
What norms are helping or hurting our culture?
If a new person joined, how would they describe our vibe?
What traditions or rituals could we start to strengthen identity?

## 10. Future Focus and Continuous Improvement

What's our next evolution as a team?
If we keep doing what we're doing, where will we be in six months?
What's one experiment we could try to level up?
What's no longer serving us?
What would make our team 10 percent better?

# ENDNOTES

1   Stanley McChrystal et al., *Team of Teams: New Rules of Engagement for a Complex World* (New York: Portfolio/Penguin, 2015).

2   "Google Re:Work - Guides: Understand Team Effectiveness," Google, accessed February 4, 2026, https://rework.withgoogle. com/intl/en/guides/understanding-team-effectiveness.

3   Amy Edmondson, "Psychological Safety and Learning Behavior in Work Teams," *Administrative Science Quarterly* 44, no. 2 (June 1999): 350–83, https://doi.org/10.2307/2666999.

4   Ryan Pendell, "Employee Engagement Strategies: Fixing the World's $8.8 Trillion Problem," Gallup.com, September 8, 2025, https://www.gallup.com/workplace/393497/world-trillion-workplace-problem.aspx.

5   Harry Markowitz, "Portfolio Selection," *The Journal of Finance* 7, no. 1 (1952): 77–91.

6   Markowitz, "Portfolio Selection."

7   Alejandro Krell et al., "How Strategy Champions Win," McKinsey & Company, July 14, 2025, https://www.mckinsey. com/capabilities/strategy-and-corporate-finance/our-insights/ how-strategy-champions-win.

8   Gallup, *State of the Global Workplace* (Washington, DC: Gallup Press, 2023).

9   Amy C. Edmondson, *The Fearless Organization: Creating Psychological Safety in the Workplace for Learning, Innovation, and Growth* (Hoboken, NJ: John Wiley & Sons, 2018).

10  Deloitte Insights, *Diversity and Inclusion: The Reality Gap* (2017), https://www2.deloitte.com/us/en/insights/focus/ human-capital-trends/2017/diversity-and-inclusion-at-the-workplace.html.

11  Korn Ferry, "How Diverse Teams Increase Innovation and Growth," Korn Ferry Institute, 2023, https://www.kornferry. com/insights/featured-topics/diversity-equity-inclusion/ how-diverse-teams-increase-innovation-and-growth.

12  Zippia.com, "Wealth Management Advisor Demographics and Statistics in the US," 2023, https://www.zippia.com/ wealth-management-advisor-jobs/demographics/.

13  CECP, "Diversity & Inclusion in Corporate Social Engagement," Chief Executives for Corporate Purpose, 2018, https://cecp.co/wp-content/uploads/2018/12/cecp_di_ whitepaper_FINAL.pdf.

14  Ibrahim Bouchrika, "Why Is There Still a Lack of Diversity in Tech?," Zippia.com, 2024, https://www.zippia.com/ why-is-there-still-a-lack-of-diversity-in-tech/.

15  Deloitte Insights, *Diversity and Inclusion*, 2017.

16  Patrick M. Lencioni, *The Five Dysfunctions of a Team* (San Francisco: Jossey-Bass, 2002).

17  John H. Zenger, Joe Folkman, and Scott K. Edinger, *The Inspiring Leader: Unlocking the Secrets of How Extraordinary Leaders Motivate* (New York, NY: McGraw Hill, 2009).

18  McChrystal et al., *Team of Teams*.

19  Jon R. Katzenbach and Douglas K. Smith, *The Wisdom of Teams: Creating the High-Performance Organization* (Boston: Harvard Business Review Press, 2015).

20  *Stanford Executive Coaching Survey*, 2013, https://www.gsb. stanford.edu/sites/gsb/files/publication-pdf/cgri-survey-2013- executive-coaching.pdf.

21  Hieu Minh Vu, "Employee Empowerment and Empowering Leadership: A Literature Review," *Technium: Romanian Journal of Applied Sciences and Technology* 2, no. 7 (2020): 20–28, https://doi.org/10.47577/technium.v2i7.1653valued, given the opportunity to continually develop and contribute to the team in more meaningful ways beyond .

22  Stephen R. Covey, *The 7 Habits of Highly Effective People* (New York: Simon & Schuster, 1989).

23  Pendell, "Employee Engagement Strategies."

24  James C. Collins, *Good to Great: Why Some Companies Make the Leap ... and Others Don't* (New York, NY: Collins, 2009).

25  Gallup, *Leadership & Management: Employee Trust in Organizational Leadership* (2024), https://www.gallup.com.

26  Carolyn Crist, "Employers See $7 ROI for Every $1 Spent on Leadership Programs, Report Says," *HR Dive*, 2023, https://www.hrdive.com/news/employers-see-7-roi-for-every-1-spent-on-leadership-programs-report-says/635177/.

27  A. J. Hampton, A. N. Fisher Boyd, and S. Sprecher, "You're Like Me and I Like You: Mediators of the Similarity–Liking Link," *Journal of Social and Personal Relationships* 36, no. 7 (2019): 2221–2244, https://doi.org/10.1177/0265407518790411.

28  Colin Baker, "What Is Transformational Leadership?," Leaders.com, updated January 5, 2023, https://leaders.com/articles/leadership/transformational-leadership/.

29  Irene M. Nembhard and Amy C. Edmondson, "Making It Safe: The Effects of Leader Inclusiveness and Team Psychological Safety," *Journal of Organizational Behavior* 27, no. 7 (2006): 941–966.

30  Ron Carucci, "One More Time: Why Diversity Leads to Better Team Performance," *Forbes*, January 24, 2024, https://www.forbes.com/sites/roncarucci/2024/01/24/one-more-time-why-diversity-leads-to-better-team-performance/.

31  Timothy R. Clark, *The 4 Stages of Psychological Safety: Defining the Path to Inclusion and Innovation* (Oakland, CA: Berrett-Koehler Publishers, Inc, 2020).

32  Outside the team development space, psychologists have used this concept of an upward spiral to promote mental health at an individual level. See, for example: Andrea B. Burns et al., "Upward Spirals of Positive Emotion and Coping: Replication, Extension, and Initial Exploration of Neurochemical Substrates," *Personality and Individual Differences* 44, no. 2 (January 2008): 360–70, https://doi.org/10.1016/j.paid.2007.08.015; Alex Korb and Daniel J. Siegel, *The Upward Spiral: Using Neuroscience to Reverse the Course of Depression, One Small Change at a Time* (Oakland, CA: New Harbinger Publications, Inc, 2025).

33  Scott Fulford, "Return to Office? How COVID-19 and Remote Work Reshaped the Economy.," Princeton University, May 30, 2023, https://press.princeton.edu/ideas/

return-to-office-how-covid-19-and-remote-work-reshaped-the-economy?srsltid=AfmBOoqTlMF2SsEeFDFKQIYM3W ZTXiYatNl-Nf1ha0T14DMrg3n9ATU8.

34 McLean & Company, "Employees Feel Disconnected from Their Organization's Vision and Mission: New Research from McLean & Company," PR Newswire: press release distribution, targeting, monitoring and marketing, September 6, 2023, https://www.prnewswire.com/news-releases/employees-feel-disconnected-from-their-organizations-vision-and-mission-new-research-from-mclean--company-301919411.html.

35 Simon Sinek, "How Great Leaders Inspire Action," TEDxPuget Sound (TED talk, September 2009), filmed at TED, May 4, 2010, YouTube video, 18:04, https://www.youtube.com/watch?v=qp0HIF3SfI4.

36 Sinek.

37 Violeta Robiak and Matej Mesko, "The Importance of Vision and Mission for Organizational Growth and Development," paper presented at the *Challenges of Globalization in Economics and Business: III International Scientific Conference*, Faculty of Economics and Business, Ivane Javakhishvili Tbilisi State University, Tbilisi, Georgia, 2018.

38 Carol S. Dweck, *Mindset: The New Psychology of Success* (New York: Random House, 2006).

39 Rob Desimone, "Improve Work Performance with a Focus on Employee Development," *Gallup Workplace Insights*, January 2024, https://www.gallup.com/workplace/269405/high-performanceit remains relevant-workplaces-differently.aspx.

40 Stephen R. Covey, *The 7 Habits of Highly Effective People: Powerful Lessons in Personal Change* (New York: Simon & Schuster, 1989).

41 Benjamin Harkin et al., "Does Monitoring Goal Progress Promote Goal Attainment? A Meta-Analysis of the Experimental Evidence.," *Psychological Bulletin* 142, no. 2 (February 2016): 198–229, https://doi.org/10.1037/bul0000025.

42 Teresa Amabile and Steven Kramer, *The Progress Principle: Using Small Wins to Ignite Joy, Engagement, and Creativity at Work* (Boston, MA: Harvard Business Review Press, 2011).

43 Gallup, Inc., "State of the American Workplace."

44 Covey, *7 Habits of Highly Effective People.*

45 Russell L. Ackoff, *The Democratic Corporation: A Radical Prescription for Recreating Corporate America and Rediscovering Success* (New York: Oxford University Press, 1994).

46 Phil Fersht, David Ryan, and R. Rajagopalan, *Bad Data Is Killing Your Business Transformation Efforts: A C-Suite Guide to Stop Talking and Start Doing* (HFS Research, 2021).

47 Covey, *7 Habits of Highly Effective People.*

48 Chris McChesney, Sean Covey, and Jim Huling, *The 4 Disciplines of Execution: Achieving Your Wildly Important Goals* (New York, NY: Free Press, 2016).

49 Joana Barsh and Johanne Mogelof, "Time Management: Your Scarcest Resource," *McKinsey Quarterly*, 2015, https://www.mckinsey.com/featured-insights/leadership/time-management-your-scarcest-resource.

50 Rasmus Benson-Armer, Steve Noble, and Sarah Dinger, *The Alignment Advantage* (Bain & Company, 2020).

51 John Doerr and Larry Page, *Measure What Matters: How Google, Bono, and the Gates Foundation Rock the World with Okrs* (NY, NY: Portfolio/Penguin, 2018).

52 Joseph A. Allen et al., "Why Am I so Exhausted?," *Journal of Occupational & Environmental Medicine* 64, no. 12 (July 18, 2022): 1053–58, https://doi.org/10.1097/jom.0000000000002641.

53 RescueTime, *The State of Knowledge Work 2019* (2019), https://rescuetime.com/knowledge-work.

54 Bevins, F., & De Smet, A. (2013). *Making time management the organization's priority.* McKinsey Quarterly.

55 "Workplace Woes: Meetings," Work Life by Atlassian, January 9, 2025, https://www.atlassian.com/blog/workplace-woes-meetings.

56 University of North Carolina. (2019). Meetings and Task Completion Study. Chapel Hill, NC: UNC Kenan-Flagler Business School.

57 Michael Mankins and Eric Garton, "Meetings: How to Make Them Matter," *Bain & Company Insight*, 2016.

58 Joseph E. Mroz et al., "Do We Really Need Another Meeting? The Science of Workplace Meetings," *Current Directions in*

*Psychological Science* 27, no. 6 (October 19, 2018): 484–91, https://doi.org/10.1177/0963721418776307.

59   Lencioni, *Five Dysfunctions of a Team.*

60   Edmondson, "Psychological Safety and Learning Behavior."

61   Anita Williams Woolley, Christopher F. Chabris, Alex Pentland, Nada Hashmi, and Thomas W. Malone, "Evidence for a Collective Intelligence Factor in the Performance of Human Groups," *Science* 330, no. 6004 (October 29, 2010): 686–688, https://doi.org/10.1126/science.1193147.

62   Edmondson, "Psychological Safety and Learning Behavior."

63   Lencioni, *Five Dysfunctions of a Team.*

64   Charles Duhigg, *Smarter Faster Better: The Secrets of Being Productive in Life and Business* (New York: Random House, 2016).

65   Edmondson, "Psychological Safety and Learning Behavior."

66   Kim Scott, *Radical Candor: Be a Kick-Ass Boss Without Losing Your Humanity* (New York: St. Martin's Press, 2017).

67   International Coaching Federation, *2023 Global Coaching Study* (Lexington, KY: International Coaching Federation, 2023), https://coachingfederation.org/resources/research/global-coaching-study/.

68   Charles Duhigg, "What Google Learned From Its Quest to Build the Perfect Team," *New York Times*, February 25, 2016. (This article explains how psychological safety was identified as the top factor for high-performing teams by Project Aristotle.)

69   Edmondson, "Psychological Safety and Learning Behavior."

70   Timothy A. Judge and Ronald F. Piccolo, "Transformational and Transactional Leadership: A Meta-Analytic Test of Their Relative Validity," *Journal of Applied Psychology* 89, no. 5 (2004): 755–68.

71   Moonsun Kim, Robert Eisenberger, and Kyunghee Baik, "Perceived Organizational Support and Prosocial Behavior: The Role of Leader–Member Exchange and Organizational Justice," *Journal of Applied Psychology* 103, no. 6 (2018): 662–70.

72   International Coaching Federation, *2023 Global Coaching Study.*

73   Richard Boyatzis, Melvin Smith, and Ellen Van Oosten, *Helping People Change: Coaching with Compassion for Lifelong*

*Learning and Growth* (Boston: Harvard Business Review Press, 2019).

74  Center for Creative Leadership, *The Role of Coaching in Leadership Development* (Colorado Springs, CO: CCL White Paper, 2020).

75  Antonios Theodosiou and Athanasios Papaioannou, "Leadership and Coaching: Meta-Analysis of Coach Behaviors," *Journal of Applied Sport Psychology* 34, no. 3 (2022): 211–230.

76  McKinsey & Company, "Building Capabilities for Performance," 2023, https://www.mckinsey.com/capabilities/people-and-organizational-performance/our-insights.

77  Amy Edmondson, "Psychological Safety and Learning Behavior in Work Teams," Administrative Science Quarterly 44, no. 2 (June 1999): 354, doi.org.

78  Edmondson, *The Fearless Organization*.

79  Gallup, *State of the Global Workplace: 2023 Report* (Washington, DC: Gallup, 2023), PDF.

80  Center for Creative Leadership, WORK 3.0: Reimagining Leadership in a Hybrid World, Research Report (Greensboro, NC: Center for Creative Leadership, 2022), https://www.ccl.org/wp-content/uploads/2022/11/work-3-reimagining-leadership-in-a-hybrid-world-research-report-cc.pdf.

81  Chris Ernst and Donna Chrobot-Mason, *Boundary Spanning Leadership: Six Practices for Solving Problems, Driving Innovation, and Transforming Organizations* (New York, NY: McGraw-Hill, 2011).

82  Daniel Goleman, *Working with Emotional Intelligence* (New York: Bantam, 1998).

83  Daniel Coyle, *The Culture Code: The Secrets of Highly Successful Groups* (New York: Bantam, 2018).

84  Edgar H. Schein, *Organizational Culture and Leadership*, 4th ed. (San Francisco: Jossey-Bass, 2010).

85  Alex "Sandy" Pentland, "The New Science of Building Great Teams," *Harvard Business Review* 90, no. 4 (2012): 60–69.

# ABOUT THE AUTHORS

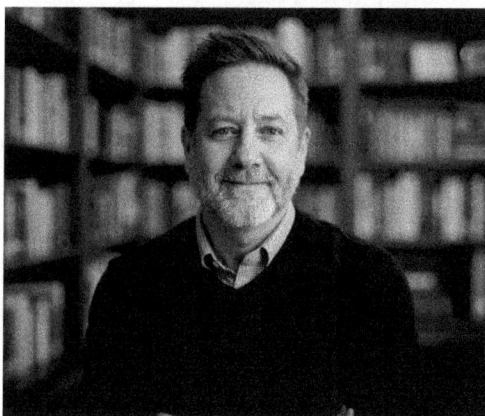

## Bryan Powell, MS, PCC, CPBA

*Executive Leadership & Team Coach | CEO –*
*Executive Coaching Space*

### About Bryan

Bryan Powell is an executive leadership and team coach who partners with senior executives, emerging leaders, and high-performing teams to unlock potential, accelerate growth, and deliver measurable business results. His driving purpose—his "Why"—is to help leaders see the greatness within themselves so they can unleash it fully in service of their organizations and communities.

## Background & Experience

With more than 4,000 hours of documented coaching experience, Bryan has guided leaders at every stage of their careers, from rising managers to C-suite executives. He has served as an internal executive coach for Fortune 100 companies, including Wells Fargo, Merrill Lynch, and Crown Castle, where his coaching directly supported business transformation, leadership effectiveness, and team performance.

Bryan is also a recognized thought leader, contributing to the Forbes Coaches Council, where he shares actionable insights and strategies to help leaders and teams consistently perform at a high level.

Beyond his client work, Bryan is deeply committed to advancing the coaching profession and his community, providing pro bono coaching to Nonprofit organizations to help them develop their team skills as they serve the communities where we work and live.

## Coaching Philosophy

Bryan's coaching is anchored in trust, authenticity, and measurable results. He leverages a diverse toolkit, including Intelligent Leadership, The 5 Behaviors of a Cohesive Team, DISC, Motivators, Stakeholder-Centered 360 Coaching, and advanced Team Coaching methodologies, to adapt to each client's unique needs.

His approach blends quantitative metrics (ROI, performance outcomes) with qualitative insights (engagement, culture, mindset) to ensure lasting impact. Leaders working with Bryan consistently report breakthroughs in clarity, collaboration, and performance.

## Education & Credentials

**MS in Organizational Leadership** – Colorado State University

**BS in Economics** – California State University, Long Beach

**Pursuing a PhD in Performance Psychology**

**Professional Certified Coach (PCC)** – International Coaching Federation

## Thomas Reynolds

Tom is a seasoned coach and designer who works across industries and around the globe to develop leaders and transform teams. He is a business psychologist who spent seven years honing his craft in Deloitte Consulting's Leadership Practice. He then spent two years in-house at Crown Castle, Inc., where he and Bryan started thinking about how to disrupt the team development space.

In 2024, Tom established his own boutique consultancy, Leadership for the Long Term. He believes in a highly practical approach to designing development solutions that go beyond one-act performative exercises and instead set the stage for enduring transformation over the long term. Currently, he serves clients across the professional services, manufacturing, life sciences, and financial services industries.

He has a doctorate in clinical psychology and an MBA from Widener University. A husband, dad, and stepdad, he lives just outside Boston, Massachusetts, where he enjoys hiking with his golden retriever mix when he has the time. He also coaches both his kids in basketball and soccer. At home and at work, he is intentional about bringing a sense of balance, commitment, and passion to everything he does.

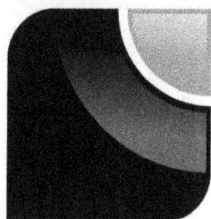